Millionaire

Millionaire

Al Winnikoff

Wayne Wagner

RENAISSANCE BOOKS

Los Angeles

Library of Congress Catalog Card Number: 00-110362
ISBN: 1-58063-193-2

10 9 8 7 6 5 4 3 2 1

Published by Renaissance Books
Distributed by St. Martin's Press
Manufactured in the United States of America
First edition

If you don't know where you're going, any road will get you there.

Chinese fortune cookie

Contents

Millionaire

Introduction

You have a choice: You can choose to be rich or choose to be poor. Since you are reading this book, it's a safe bet you'd rather be rich.

If you enjoy being poor, however, please put this book down immediately and seek fulfillment elsewhere.

We too have tasted poverty—and we have tasted riches.

What's our opinion? No comparison.

What Do the Authors Know About Making You Rich?

Wayne Wagner Introduces Al Winnikoff

Cliffside Drive is one of the most exclusive streets in Malibu. Movie stars, business hotshots, and recording artists live there. Last year the lowest-priced house on the street sold for $2.5 million.

Al Winnikoff lives on Cliffside Drive. You can look him up in the phone book. His four-bedroom house, on an acre of land, sits on a bluff overlooking the magnificent Pacific Ocean. On a clear day, he can see Catalina Island.

Al paid $64,000 for this house. Of course that was thirty years ago, but it brings home the whole point of this book:

If you save systematically and invest carefully, time will make you a millionaire.

But Al still acts like a man who lives in a $64,000 house. As I write this, his car is parked on the street in front of my office so he doesn't have to pay for parking. How do you think he holds on to his money?

Frugality is the first trait you need. Patience is the second.

Al sells houses for a living. In a good year he can peddle $50,000,000 worth of real estate. In a bad year? Zip. So he is literally forced to save during the good times in order to stay alive in the bad. His real estate philosophy is simple: (1) Brace yourself for the bad times, because they are always coming, and (2) Buy and never sell.

He knows with certainty that if he sells you a house in Malibu today, and it is geologically stable, you will be a millionaire in twenty-five years if you hang on to it. But not everyone can do this today, which is why this book isn't about real estate. Al started buying properties in Malibu in the 1960s, when prices were within reach of the average person's grasp. That is no longer the case.

This book is for people starting out today, which is where Al was thirty years ago. It will explain in detail precisely how to make a million dollars in the next twenty-five years with very little effort on your part.

Al Winnikoff Introduces Wayne Wagner

When I first met Wagner, he told me he was short on money but long on promise. I believed him.

What I sensed in Wayne was a kindred spirit—a man who did not understand failure. Did not, could not, and would not. Setbacks? Certainly. Failure? Never. Success? Inevitable.

I sold him his first ocean-view residence in Malibu twenty-five years ago with no money down.

Since that time, he founded a financial advisory firm, the Plexus Group, which advises money managers, corporations, and brokerage firms on cost-effective money management. The firm, which has thirty-seven employees, advises clients who manage $1.5 trillion in assets for their clients worldwide. You can look Wayne up on the Internet at Plexusgroup.com.

> **It's easy to succeed, but most investors don't know that— and they don't succeed.**

Wayne Wagner began his career with nothing but a great sense of optimism and a ten-year-old Ford. But he sure knew his business, and he sure knew how to save money. And he sure knows when, where, and how to invest it.

In addition to being one of the world's leading financial advisors, Wayne plays the guitar and sings poorly. He looks like a failed folk singer of the '60s ought to look: thinning hair, slight paunch, dusty guitar, and unexceptional voice. (Wayne's motto is "If you can't sing good, sing loud.") It's a good thing he found his calling in the business world.

In his forty years in the investment business, Wayne has seen many professional managers succeed and many fail. He's also seen many investors fail to meet their goals, and a few of them succeed. Wayne has come to the conclusion that it's easy to succeed, but most investors don't know that—and they don't succeed.

We've talked about the first two traits you need to become a millionaire—frugality and patience. That brings us to the third necessary trait—the ability to invest carefully. In one sentence: Keep saving, take risk, buy a lot of different things, and keep your taxes and expenses low, low, low.

We can actually say all of this in two words: *never sell.*

Spend an hour or two with us and you will know how—and why. Spend a lifetime applying this simple, straightforward knowledge and you will be a millionaire too.

But First, Some Serious Advice

Both of us read a lot of books for pleasure. You know the routine—read the book in bed until the book or your eyelids drop. But this book isn't one you read while half conscious. It isn't the kind of book you read for pleasure. It's more like a recipe book, like *The Joy of Cooking.* We've tried to be amusing and accessible, but the real fun starts when you get into the financial kitchen and begin to cook up a fortune for your family.

We're going to ask you to do more than just read this book. We're going to ask you to act—in your best interest, in your family's best interest, and in the interest of your own future.

Look, when you bought this book, you came to us for advice. You paid for that advice. If your doctor says that if you don't start living differently, then you're going to live miserably and die, do you ignore it? If we say that if you don't start handling your money differently, then you're going to live hand-to-mouth and die a pauper, are you going to ignore us?

We hope not.

Now that we've got your attention, you're ready for the first big secret to becoming a millionaire.

Beware of Get-Rich-Quick Schemes

Experience is the name that men give to their screw-ups.

Author unknown

You've all heard of get-rich-quick schemes, and most of the time the success stories you hear sound just too good to be true. If you really take a look at some of these so-called fool-proof deals, either the cost is just too high—too much money to lay out, too high a risk, too much stress—or there's something downright illegal hidden beneath the surface.

If you don't turn out to be one of the lucky few who come out the other side with a fortune, you could risk losing a lot more than your initial investment. So is it worth it? Consider these real-life stories.

Al wasn't always the picture of probity that all those fine words in his introduction might lead you to believe. In his younger years, he had some brushes with fast money. In the coin business, to be exact.

In the 1970s, when gold and silver reached an astronomical high, Al and his friend and former high-school partner-in-crime, Bernie Lichtman, persuaded a bank to finance their purchase of three hundred bags of silver coins. At the time, Al was earning $12,000 a year writing technical manuals for Litton Industries and slowly investing in land whenever he could. Silver seemed like a sure thing at the time. Demand was high and the price just kept climbing. If only he and Bernie could hold on to their coins for at least six or seven years, they'd be rich.

Al and Bernie got together a bunch of partners to share the cost of the loan payments and eventual profits, but it was still a struggle to make those payments. They managed to do it for two whole years, until the bank raised its interest rate on their loan. Al and Bernie were simply unable to make the higher payments. They were already stretched to their limit. They had to sell the coins.

But Al and Bernie still netted a profit of $1,500 each. Had they been able to hold on another ten years, their little profit would have become a big profit. So big, in fact, that the shrewd guy who took fifty bags of the coins off Al's hands for a modest $1,700 per bag ended up ten years later with $2.5 million for his $85,000 investment.

Years after Al unloaded the silver dollars, one of his lawyer friends called and said, "Hey, Winnikoff, you still in the coin business?"

"No."

"You know anything about Mexican 50-peso gold pieces?"

"No."

"Are you interested in 50-peso gold pieces for $400 apiece?"

"No."

"Well, here's the deal. I can buy them by the bag for $400 apiece. Is that a good deal?"

"They're selling for $800 apiece on the open market, so I'm sure it's a scam."

"Now look, Al, I'd like to have lunch and go over this with you."

"Who's paying?" Al asked.

"Well, you are, of course."

Al and Charlie Lawyer lunched at IHOP in Beverly Hills.

"Look," Charlie said, "this guy Doroteo Arango is a great cement contractor and he's done a lot of great jobs for me."

"In lieu of legal fees?" Al asked.

"Well, yeah, sort of . . . but how did you know?"

"Intuition."

"Anyway," Charlie said, "his brother-in-law is a very rich guy down in Tijuana who deals in gold coins. He's got so many of them, he has to dispose of them by the bag. Big numbers. Look, I don't know exactly why the guy's doing this, but he must have his reasons."

"Charlie, I'm telling you, it's a scam. A bag is worth $800,000 and he's selling them for $400,000? It's a scam."

"Al, look, Doroteo took all these pictures of his brother-in-law standing in a big vault with all these bags, and . . ."

"Charlie, let me tell you what I found out in ten minutes worth of phone calls. Number one, it is absolutely illegal to remove gold coins from Mexico . . ."

"Yeah, but what if he promises delivery? What if this thing's on the up and up? After all, this guy Porfirio Diaz is related to the former president."

"I still don't like it," Al said.

"Look, Al, I've defended your interests and never lost a case . . ."

"That's because I was always innocent."

"Hey, let's not argue. I've set up a meeting for next Wednesday evening. How about it?"

"Okay, I'll go. But be sure to tell your office exactly where we're going and exactly where we'll be. And when."

"Don't worry," Charlie said. "You'll be perfectly safe. After all, I'm your lawyer."

"Who's driving?" Al asked.

"Well, you are, of course."

Two days after their cheap lunch in Beverly Hills, Al, Charlie Lawyer, and Charlie's client Doroteo Arango, a cement contractor who was the Mexican go-between, went to Tijuana to seek their mighty fortune and turn dreams into instant gold. They all wore suits and ties for the occasion. This was big, important stuff.

Gold was at an all-time high, and one-ounce BU gold coins *were* selling for $800 apiece. Al knew this to be true simply by calling a large coin dealer, Superior Stamp & Coin.

"We'll buy all you've got," the dealer told him. "And, by the way, 50-peso gold pieces are not one ounce. They're 1.2 ounces each."

When the trio of Al, Charlie, and Doroteo arrived on Wednesday night at 7:00 P.M. at the home of Porfirio Diaz in Tijuana, Mexico, it was absolutely spooky.

They were instructed to drive into a gated compound where two armed guards, holding dogs on chains, waved them on to the house. The guards wore bandoleers. They were fully armed. They were not friendly.

"I'll bet this guy's never been robbed," Al said.

"Never!" Doroteo confirmed.

Señor Diaz greeted them graciously in the foyer and escorted the men into a large living room. He bubbled with enthusiasm.

Before getting down to business, Porfirio Diaz put on a great show for the visitors. He spoke good English. He told them he was sixty-five years old and had the strength and health of a twenty-year-old. He slapped his chest, arms, legs, thighs, hips, and kept saying, "Look how strong, how solid! Not bad, eh?"

"Very good," Al replied.

Men kill for this!

"I hear you are a very rich coin dealer from Malibu."

"I'm not a coin dealer. I don't own any coins at all. But I was involved about five years ago . . ."

"Aha! Then you are a coin expert."

"No, not exactly. I'm just here to see if we can make some kind of a deal. I *do* have contacts."

"Very good, Señor Winnikoff, then let me show you what I have for $400 a coin. As you requested, the bag has the mint's seal on it. It is down there on the floor, below your right hand."

Al looked down and, sure enough, the mint-sealed canvas bag was right there.

"And here, Señor, is a pair of scissors so you can cut it," Diaz said, handing him the scissors.

Al cut the bag open, put the scissors down, and then ran his fingers through the one thousand gold coins.

No matter how rich or poor, young or old, sick or healthy, you cannot but be impressed by the look and feel of gold coins slipping and sifting through your fingers. Al knew with certainty that this was the real stuff by the way the gold dust powdered his hand and stuck to his fingers.

"Men kill for this," he said.

"They fight wars! Revolutions!" Porfirio Diaz said, throwing his arms and hands out expansively.

Al looked at Charlie and Doroteo. They were entranced. They looked as though they wanted to plunge in and run the gold coins between their own fingers. If they could buy the bag for $400,000 and sell it tomorrow for $800,000, they would be rich overnight. It is a dream often dreamt.

"So what do you think?"

"I'll pay you $750 a coin. $750,000 for the bag," Winnikoff said.

Charlie and Doroteo went stark raving mad, crazy, hysterical.

"What do you mean?? Are you crazy, Winnikoff?!"

"You're going to destroy us, aren't you?? You think *this* is a scam?? Well, Winnikoff, *you're* a scam! You can't cheat us like this!!"

"Hey, you can't do this to me—I'm your lawyer!!"

When all the lunacy and shouting subsided, Mr. Diaz said to Al, "What is the meaning of this? Your friends bring you to my house and tell me you are a big, rich, honest man from Malibu who can handle a hundred bags and I believe them. What is this?"

"Mr. Diaz, please let me explain. I am not a rich man. I'm land poor. If I had to, I don't think I could come up with $5,000 in cash by noon tomorrow."

"Then why are we talking?" Diaz asked.

"Please, let me continue. I will get you certified checks for each bag, on delivery and on two conditions. Number one, each coin has to be assayed and we'll pay for that, and, number two, we have to take delivery in the United States."

"I can't give you delivery in the United States. I'm a Mexican and I only deal in Mexico. Here, look, I am an honest man and I trust you." Diaz got up from his chair, grabbed the bag of gold in both hands, and dumped it in Al's lap. "Here. Take it and pay me tomorrow. I trust you and know you will pay me."

Al put the coins back on the floor. "Mr. Diaz, there's one other way we can do this."

"Tell me, but I am telling you it is perfectly safe and honorable to put this bag in the trunk of your car and drive home with it. Perfectly safe. Take it and go."

"What are we waiting for?" the attorney asked in a voice tinged with horror. "If you want, I'll carry it out to the car."

Porfirio and Doroteo spoke rapidly in Spanish. Then Porfirio said, "We can do it by boat. I'll deliver it to you out in the ocean from my yacht."

"No," Al said, "I won't do that. But there is one other way."

"And what is the other way?" Diaz asked.

"There are two Mexican brothers who have coin stores in Ciudad Juarez and El Paso, across the border from each other. If you make delivery in Ciudad Juarez, I can pick them up in El Paso and make payment within twenty-four hours."

"Why are you being so difficult?" Diaz asked.

"Mr. Diaz," Al said, "one hundred bags will bring you $75,000,000. That's a lot of money and you can be sure I'll deliver."

"But we're only asking you for $40,000,000," Señor Diaz said. "That's the problem."

When the nonmillionaire trio hit the border, the Mexican immigration officials tore Al's car apart. They strip-searched all three men. After two hours, they were released.

Al tried to explain to Doroteo and Charlie that the border search was no coincidence. Señor Diaz made his money on a ten-percent snitch fee at the border, which is why his prices were too good to be true.

But Doroteo and Charlie were too depressed to listen or hear what was said to them. All they could think about were the instant riches that got away.

Of course, not all get-rich-quick schemes are scams or carry too high a cost. Perhaps you'll get lucky and make the big, fast bucks. Perhaps, but it's easy to see how greed can cloud judgment and lead to big financial risks.

The trouble with this approach is that it's habit forming: you always want to double up and score again. Most who pursue this approach end up with disaster after disaster.

That's why we're not suggesting you chase instant riches but that you take a slow, deliberate, careful route to becoming a millionaire.

Now we'd like to tell you the story that inspired us to write this book.

The Saga of Charley Spenditall

Your beliefs are your reality. If you don't like the reality you see, change your beliefs.

Source unknown

Back in 1976 a bright, honest, young real estate salesman by the name of Al Winnikoff showed a house for sale to a high-strung, nervous, scrap metal dealer by the name of Charley Spenditall. It was a beautiful, $300,000 home in ritzy-glitzy Malibu, and Charley *had* to have it. Charley's wife *had* to have it. Charley's kids did handsprings in the living room.

The purchase required a $60,000 down payment. Charley's parents and in-laws, recently deceased, had left the Spenditalls a little money, but for this house of their dreams they were still short $10,000 for the down payment. Even after maxing out their credit cards and borrowing from friends and relatives, $50,000 was the sum total of their investment capability. Never mind that Charley made $50,000 a year in the international scrap metals trade. Sure he worked hard. He was on the phone day and night. But Charley and his wife lived big. Expensive clothing and perfumes were her thing. His things were Brooks Brothers suits, Gucci shoes, Rolex watches, and a big, bright, brand–new, leased, yellow Cadillac. Mrs. Spenditall, being a bit more demure, drove a white one.

Al, who would receive 3 percent of the sales price if he made the sale (the other broker in the deal would receive the other 3 percent of the sales commission), figured very quickly that if he made a $9,000 commission, added in $1,000 of his savings, and loaned it to Charley, then Charley could buy the house.

So Al loaned Charley S. the $10,000, at 8 percent interest, and the deal was struck. As agreed, Charley paid off the $10,000 over a three-year period. Payments were $313.36 per month. The total three-year cost to Charley was $11,280.96. Al put it all in his savings account and picked up, approximately, another 4 percent. At the end of three years Al had $12,003.28 in the bank. Charley, as always, had nothing.

Shortly after the payoff, Charley S. called Al and frantically asked, "Al, can you lend me another ten grand?"

"Another ten grand?" said Al. "What do you need another ten grand for?"

"I have to pay my income taxes and I'm short ten grand!" It was Friday, April 13, and C.S.'s voice sounded panicky. "I *hate* the IRS!"

"Hey," Al said, "I love those guys. When I was poor, I never used to owe them anything. So now when I write them a check it reminds me of how well I'm doing."

"That proves it," C.S. said. "I always thought you were a little crazy."

"Charley, please explain to me how a guy making $50,000 a year runs short ten grand?"

"I'm not making $50,000 a year anymore—I'm making $75,000 a year!"

"And you're shy $10,000 on your taxes?"

"Yes."

"Charley, it seems to me you're doing something wrong, and since I'm not a bank, I'm not going to loan you the ten grand. But let me tell you what I will do. I'll meet you at Security Pacific National Bank [now defunct] in an hour and get you a loan. The manager is a friend of mine and I'm sure she'll do it."

She did.

Afterward Charley and Al stepped out into the bright California sunlight and Al asked, "Have you had lunch?"

"Lunch?! I need a drink!"

"I don't drink," Al said. "Let's have lunch at the Malibu Coffee Shop [now defunct]. Don't panic. I'll pick up the tab."

At lunch he said, "Charley, tell me about yourself. How does a guy making $75,000 a year wind up ten short on his taxes? Don't you save anything?"

"No," Charley Spenditall replied.

"Didn't your parents teach you to save?"

"Oh, no!" Charley exclaimed.

"What do you mean, 'Oh no!'?" Al asked. "Why didn't they teach you to save? Were they on dope or something?"

"Oh, no!" Charley replied. "My parents were straight arrows. Worked hard and spent every penny. The only thing they left me and my brothers was an old house in Dearborn, Michigan."

"But why?"

"Well," Charley said, "they were married in 1930 and their families and friends lost everything in the Great Depression. So they were told to live it up before the next depression."

"What did your dad do? Did he have a job when he got married?"

"Oh, yeah. We were rich compared to our neighbors. I guess we were pretty lucky. But my mom and dad taught me and my brothers to work hard, have a better life, and spend every dime."

"You're sure they didn't have any vices?"

"Nope. They drank a little. Smoked about a pack a day. Maybe a little more. Maybe a little less."

"What brand?" Al asked.

"Philip Morris," Charley replied. "My father's name was Philip and he thought it was sort of cute to smoke Philip Morris cigarettes. Far as I know, they smoked from 1930 to 1976. That's when they both died of lung cancer."

Didn't your parents teach you to save?

"I'm sorry," Al said, "but I want you to do me a little favor."

"What's that?" Charley Spenditall asked.

"Look, Charley, I want you to get together with your brothers and undertake a little research project for me. I want you to figure out approximately how much your mom and dad spent on cigarettes from 1930 to 1976."

"You want me to *what?*" Charley asked.

"You heard me," Al said.

"But *why?*" Charley demanded.

"Look," Al said, "I'm not exactly your enemy. I helped you buy that house, and got you the ten-grand loan . . ."

"With two days to spare until April 15," Charley interrupted.

". . . and I'm paying for lunch," Al concluded.

"Okay, but will you please tell me why? You know, Al, you're a pretty nice guy and I've always liked you, but I always thought you were a little unusual and also a little crazy."

"Thanks. But will you do it? I'll tell you why later. I'll tell you exactly why."

"Okay . . ." Charley said.

When lunch concluded, the two salesmen shook hands and went their separate ways.

Smoke, Smoke, Smoke That Cigarette

A month later, Charley Spenditall called Al and said, "We figured that from 1930 to 1976 my mom and dad spent about $33,000 for cigarettes."

Al took the information and went to a friend at one of the world's leading financial advisory firms, the Plexus Group, and said, "Wayne, if a guy by the name of Philip Spenditall had invested $769.39 a year from 1930 to 1976 in Philip Morris stock and reinvested all the dividends, how much would it have been worth in 1976? Can you run that program for me?"

"Sure," Wayne said.

The Shocking Truth

Now, ladies and gentlemen, before you turn the page and learn the truth—as to just what that money might have earned had it been put into the Philip Morris stock instead of into the company's product—we want you to first take a guess yourself.

Ready? Okay, turn the page.

An investment of $717.39 per year for forty-six years in Philip Morris stock, with the dividends reinvested, comes to

$9,736,433.03

Had the Spenditall family continued the investment for another twenty years, the stock would have appreciated to

$746,355,617.59

And all this from a mere 1.96^{1}/_2$ per day.[1]

We realize that the cost of a pack went up in price from 1930 to 1976, but $717.39 per year averages out to 1.96^{1}/_2$ per day. Not an impossible investment for the senior Spenditalls, and certainly not an impossible investment for you.

Rule #1:   **SAVE YOUR MONEY**

Rule #2:   **SAVE YOUR MONEY**

Rule #3:   **SAVE YOUR MONEY**

Rule #4:   **INVEST**

Rule #5:   **INVEST**

Rule #6:   **INVEST**

When Al and Charley had lunch together again and Al presented Charley with the data, Charley laughed in Al's face. In fact, he roared.

---

[1]The money was invested monthly, on the first day of the month, and compounded monthly. No provision was made for commissions.

Between bites, his mouth full of food, Charley berated Al with, "So, I suppose you're telling me my folks shouldn't have smoked. It was bad for their health or something."

"Not at all. I'm simply pointing out they could have done both—smoked *and* invested."

"Hey, look, Al, I don't care about the next twenty-five years. I want it *now!* Right now!"

"Charley, I deal every year with a group of people who have exactly the same attitude."

"Who?" Charley asked.

"The IRS."

You Be the Judge

Above all, we are not touting Philip Morris stock, although the return on this stock was a phenomenal 21 percent per year for forty-six years. (Thank you, smokers.)

Charley's mom and dad didn't know it, but they had the exquisite timing to start smoking and/or investing at the market low after the 1929 crash and died just after a good run-up in Philip Morris stock in the early 1970s.

We are not touting *any* particular stock. In fact one of these authors, Al Winnikoff, does not own any stock whatsoever. He doesn't need to. He chose to invest in Malibu real estate back when prices were actually affordable, and he made a fortune. Both authors are successful in their own businesses and have made fortunes for their investors and customers. And, in a few cases, *great fortunes*.

Wayne's specialty is investing in stocks. This book will lay out a safe, slow, and sure investment program that essentially involves investing in very large numbers of stocks—*permanently*—instead of trying to pick the hot one of the day or week.

Regardless, whether we invest in stocks or in real estate, we know the value of investing steadily, safely, conservatively, and for the long haul. It matters not whether you are rich, poor, black, white, yellow, red, or green. You, too, can do it if you set your mind to it.

Go your own way and make your own deal.

Take advice from no one. Not even us. Sure, we believe our advice will make you rich, but you still must do it all on your own. We can give you the key, but your brain is the lock.

When Eugene B. Eagerbeaver, your next-door neighbor, tells you to buy America Online because he's made a fortune in it, simply smile. After-the-fact free advice is worth exactly what you pay for it. Forget about all the people in the world who give or sell advice.

Go your own way and make your own deal. Believe in yourself and your own future.

In 2000 there were approximately seven million families in the U.S. that were millionaire families. In 2005 there will be approximately ten million families that will be millionaire families.

And your family eventually will be one of them. Believe it and be there. Be there with a positive optimism. Be there with a great love for your family in your heart.

Just be there.

Introducing
. . . the Index Fund

Not doing more than average is what keeps the average down.

Source unknown

We'll let you in on a little secret before we go any further. It's really simple. Anyone can become a millionaire. Just save your money every month—we'll tell you how much—and put it in a good *index fund*. That's it!

What is an index fund? Think of it as a very large number of stocks packaged together so you can buy and sell them as a unit. Sound like a mutual fund? Actually, an index fund is quite different.

Unlike a traditional mutual fund, an index fund does not try to beat the market; in essence, it *is* the market. Instead of relying on mutual fund managers to buy and sell the right combination of stocks, an index fund simply replicates the daily ups and downs of a given index, such as the Standard & Poor's (S&P) 500 or the Dow Jones industrial average—which are barometers of how the stock market is doing on any given day.

How does an index fund replicate a given index? By holding all the stocks in the index in the right proportion. Because the index fund is simply a mirror of a given index, managing it is really a non-issue, especially when compared with what it takes to run a mutual fund. Don't be fooled by the index fund's simplicity, however. The index fund, which invests via computer control and not via human control, has whipped the financial socks off mutual funds for the better part of the last two decades.

The superior performance of the index fund isn't about lucky breaks; the index fund is a better bet than the mutual fund because it is a low-cost, low-tax investment that reflects the enduring strength of the American economy. And, while no investment is risk-free, the index fund's holdings—in a broad range of solid, dependable companies—reduces that risk considerably.

Once you pick an index fund and start contributing to it every month, all you have to do is just sit back and let time do the rest. It's a low-maintenance, proven investment that won't let you down. It may not be as sexy as picking individual stocks, placing adrenaline-charged calls to your broker, or trading on the Internet, but it's a lot more likely to put those six zeros on the end of your bank balance while you're still around to enjoy them.

Later on we'll discuss index funds in detail and why they're your surest path to millionairedom. We'll compare them with all the other different types of investments that are available to you, and we'll make it all easy to understand.

But first we need to introduce you to a few essential principles that all millionaires-in-training must learn.

Save Your Money

Ninety percent of success is simply showing up.

Woody Allen, comedian

We want you to be a millionaire. Not by luck or fluke or mistake or marriage, but by design—by taking control of your destiny, screwing up your courage, rolling up your sleeves, and biting the bullet. Once you have taken the initiative, follow our directions and we *promise* you that, if you give us the time, we will *absolutely* make you a millionaire.

The time you must give us is twenty-five years of your life. Maybe more, maybe less. Many will scoff at this twenty-five-year span, but guess where they will be in twenty-five years.

You, on the other hand, will save your money, pay close attention, and find yourself quite wealthy in the next quarter century. You must never be cynical or use the ugly, ugly words, "Yeah, but what if . . ."

There is, as you read these words, an ambitious immigrant crossing our borders in pursuit of a low-paying job and a better future than he had in his home country. Twenty-five years later, the guy's a millionaire and everyone who knows the guy (including the IRS) wants to know: *How did he do it?*

We will tell you exactly how he did it. *He saved his money.*

Now, we must impress this very simple lesson upon you if you are to become a millionaire. You *must* follow these three basic but simple rules:

Rule #1:   **SAVE YOUR MONEY**

Rule #2:   **SAVE YOUR MONEY**

Rule #3:   **SAVE YOUR MONEY**

You must do this without fail and without complaint. We don't care if you make $10,000 a year or more than $100,000. To become a millionaire, you must *save your money, save your money, save your money.*

Our critics will pooh-pooh our advice, but in all of human history no one has ever built a monument to a critic. And very few critics die millionaires.

Dare to Be Different

Many of the people who deal with Al Winnikoff think he's not just eccentric but also completely bonkers. Nonetheless, Al is respected by the banking community.

To say the least, he is a preferred customer at Northern Trust Bank. When Al mentioned to one of the bank's vice presidents that he still does a lot of his own plumbing and fixes his own toilets, the v.p. said, "You whaaat? Why would you do a thing like that?"

"It saves me money."

Folks might laugh at Al for his eccentricities but, unlike Al, they're not laughing all the way to the bank.

One time Al was purchasing some supplies at West L.A. Electrical, which has a long counter that accommodates twenty customers at a time as well as probably twenty salespeople. Yaakov, the owner, was trying to talk Al into a hot electrical deal in Russia. Sorry, Yaakov. Not interested.

In *your* life, *you* call the tune.

"Yaakov," Al said loudly, "there are only three things you have to know to become a millionaire in this country."

The salescounter became suddenly silent.

Forty pairs of eyes and ears were upon Winnikoff in a flash. West L.A. Electrical came to a shocking halt.

Al continued: "Number one, save your money. Number two, save your money. And number three, save your money."

At that point everyone went back to buying and selling sockets, switches, and circuits. And where will that gang be in twenty-five years? Selling and buying sockets, switches, and circuits at West L.A. Electrical, that's where.

As Al was paying for his supplies, the cashier said to him, "Say, haven't I seen your signs around? Aren't you in real estate?"

"Yes."

"Hey, Mr. Winnikoff, could you maybe give me a job or something? Help me out, sort of? I can't save any money on this job."

"Another fallacy, young man. If you can't save it *here,* you can't save it *anywhere.*"

Al wasn't being condescending. He knew the guy probably wasn't earning a lot. But saving is not just a matter of having more money than you need. How many of us ever have more money than we think we need?

What you have to decide is what you really want. Do you want a lot of new stuff? Do you want lunch? Or do you want to be a millionaire? Saving is a mind-set. If you only have a little, you save a little. If you have a lot, you save a lot.

But if you have the mind-set that you can't save any money, then there's always someone or something else to blame it on. You can blame it on tough breaks or bad luck, or you can blame it on your rotten childhood when your parents or probation officer told you that you were worthless and would never amount to anything. Kids really do believe that kind of stuff. They may not listen when their parents say, on a freezing winter's day, "Shut the door!" or "Close the window!" But tell kids they're worthless, irresponsible, or any other negative trait, and they'll hear it loud and clear. That's why they learn to make up excuses like "the dog vomited on my homework."

But for adults, and especially the adult readers of this book, poor excuses will not wash (just try telling your boss the dog vomited on your homework). Like it or not, believe it or not, the fact remains that in *your* life, *you* call the tune. You get to be responsible for how you live your life.

Case in point: Back in 1947, when Al was a student at Fremont High School in South Central L.A., the vice principal was an ogre hated by one and all, especially smokers whom he expelled right and left. Al exercised his First Amendment rights and wrote a brilliant, open letter to the vice principal on the matter of smoking.

Al's best friend, Bernie Lichtman, let Al use his mimeograph machine to let the world know what a jerk Mr. Costello was. After distribution of the letter, the righteous authorities kicked these hoodlums out, and everyone from the superintendent of schools down to the janitor told them they were no-good, rotten kids and would never amount to anything.

But they did anyway. Bernie's company, The Lichtman Company, is one of the world's leading stamp wholesalers. And as for Al, you already know how well he's done for himself.

No matter what kind of struggles you've had in the past, or what your parents, teachers, or friends said you could or couldn't achieve, you *can* break out of your old self-image and turn yourself from a spender into a saver.

What Separates the Savers from the Spenders

According to *Money* magazine (August 2000), there are approximately 100,000,000 families in the U.S. Of these, as noted earlier, approximately 7,000,000 are millionaire families. Of the 7,000,000, 80 percent, or 5,600,000, are self-made millionaires.

This is an amazing statistic; indeed it is a first in human history. Even more astounding than the percentages and numbers is the fact that most American millionaires

- are plain, ordinary, down-to-earth sorts who do not flaunt their wealth;
- look and act and talk and eat and sleep pretty much like the rest of us;
- are modest and not interested in showy displays of wealth;

- live by the rules of hard work and perseverance;
- act much the same after attaining millionaire status as they did before;
- are self-employed, confident, and know how to mind their own business;
- have good, stable family lives;
- have a superb credit rating; and
- like the proverbial British diplomat, they pursue an attainable goal with great singularity of purpose.

The lunatics and losers who make up a large percentage of the nation's other 93,000,000 families take this approach to minding someone else's business: "Hey, wow, man, if I had your money I'd buy me a . . ."

We all know exactly how the sentence ends. The massive difference between the savers and spenders is readily apparent.

- The savers understand us and we understand them.
- The savers know the secret of success: There is no secret. It's all a matter of grit and guts.
- The savers will heed our words.
- The savers live life with optimism in their hearts.
- The savers put money in the bank.
- The savers will find success.

No use talking to the spenders.

- The spenders will find failure.
- The spenders live life with criticism on their lips.
- The spenders spend every dime, go into debt, and, over a twenty-five-year span, will search the world over for that great big monument to a famous critic.

So, please—pay attention. Pay the bill. Ignore the naysayers. Dare to be different. And save your money. Not tomorrow, or next payday, or with a New Year's resolution. Do it now. Because you're worth it. And, if nothing else, think of how happy these authors will be to know that their book is not just a success, but a *great success*—for they will have created yet another budding millionaire.

Invest Your Money

Semper vult mundis decipi: decipietur.
The world always wishes to be deceived; let it be deceived.

Oxenstierana, philosopher

Now that we have bludgeoned you with the first three rules and the importance of saving your money, we will go on to the next set of important rules:

Rule #4:   **INVEST**

Rule #5:   **INVEST**

Rule #6:   **INVEST**

There are simple but powerful reasons for following these rules, because in the financial arena the only law of economics that always prevails is the law of (1) *supply* and (2) *demand*.

Which means that in economics there are only two types of people: (1) *producers* and (2) *consumers.*

The consumers are the people who would rather give up their money than their fantasies. That's when chain letters, pyramid schemes, and Ponzi types destroy the smooth operation of the marketplace. Ever heard of Charles Ponzi? He made a racket out of paying investors 10 percent interest per month.

How did he do that? Well, he paid his first investors 10 percent, just like he promised. The problem was, however, that the company hadn't actually earned anything—Ponzi just paid them out of the money that they themselves had invested. But when they received their checks, word got out and in no time people were beating down his door to invest in his company.

When the scheme gained momentum, Ponzi was taking in so much money that his untrained staff had to stuff the incoming dollars into trash cans. As new investors put in their money, Ponzi used it not to build the company but to pay himself handsomely and to keep up his interest payments. Naturally, the investors who had gotten *their* interest payments figured the company was a success, so they dumped those earnings back into Ponzi's scheme.

Then it happened. Ponzi ran out of enough new investors to pay off the old, there was no real business to support it, and the whole thing collapsed. New investors, old investors, they all lost everything. For a brief period in his troubled life Charlie Ponzi lived big, rich, and happy. But by the end, he went to jail and died a pauper.

Obviously Ponzi was an out-and-out crook. But the investors weren't. They were just ordinary people who thought they were putting their money into a good thing. After all, this wasn't like the guy who tried to get Al to illegally buy gold coins. This was a real company. Probably had letterhead and everything.

And that's the point—not all scams are as blatantly illegal as the gold-coin deal. Like Ponzi's scheme, the good ones have all the trappings of a real investment. And some of Ponzi's investors did make money. If you got in early enough, cashed out, and stayed out, it would have been a good investment. But most people couldn't resist the temptation to stay in when they thought they were getting such a good return on their money.

The lesson is, if a deal looks too good to be true, then it probably is. The same can be true in the stock market, the real estate market, and even the produce market. You don't believe us? Then go study the tulipomania craze that struck Holland in the 1620s, when the tulip was a new and exotic flower there. In Charles MacKay's 1841 book titled *Extraordinary Popular Delusions and the Madness of Crowds,* he reported that the bulbs were so precious that *one* Viceroy tulip bulb was sold for:

- 2 lasts of wheat (1 last equals 2,000 pounds)
- 4 lasts of rye
- 4 fat oxen
- 8 fat swine
- 12 fat sheep
- 2 hogsheads of wine (1 hogshead equals 63 gallons)
- 4 tuns of beer (1 tun equals 252 gallons)
- 2 tuns of butter
- 1,000 pounds of cheese
- 1 bed
- 1 silver drinking cup

When the tulipomania crash came in 1637, Holland, which had been an extremely rich and powerful nation in the mid-seventeenth century, came close to complete economic collapse.

Now, tulipomania wasn't like Ponzi. It wasn't a scam. In fact, tulips were a good investment. Good, that is, as long as someone else wanted them enough to give you more silver cups and lasts of wheat than you paid for them. It only became a bad investment the day Helga woke up and said, "Y'know, Ruben, tulips are okay, but I think geraniums would be nice around the windmill."

Who knew the market was going to go bad? More to the point, who knew *when* it was going to go bad? It doesn't matter whether it's tulips or dot-coms—if you put all of your eggs in one basket, we think you're taking too big a risk.

So what's the answer? Here we are advising you to *invest, invest, invest* and then we tell you stories about people losing their shirts on bad investments. What should you do?

Remember Ruben the tulip guy? If he had also invested some of his guilders in geraniums instead of putting everything into tulips, he would have had a much better chance of surviving the crash. Better still, if he was also into wooden shoes, windmills, and dykes, he might not have even felt it. Ruben would have spread his risk. That's what we advise you to do. And, as we said earlier, the best way to do it is to invest in an index fund.

So, yes, *invest, invest, invest*—but invest wisely. And do it now.

Do It Now

In 1954 Al went into the laundry business with his dad, Morris Winnikoff. Al put in $3,000, his dad put in $12,000, the Bank of America loaned them $10,000, and they purchased the La Tijera Washette in Westchester, California. Full price, $25,000. Al was twenty-four years old.

By 1956 Al and his dad had paid off the $10,000 bank loan *twice*. They did this first by doubling up the payments on the $10,000 two-year loan so that they paid it off in one year. For this, the bank loved them. So they borrowed $10,000 again and paid it off by the following year.

Now, instead of zero dollars in the bank they had $10,000, and they each took wages of $75 per week. A few years later, with no more debt, they sold the business for exactly what they paid originally: $25,000. Instead of their original $15,000 net worth, they now had a $35,000 net worth. This was after they paid all their city, county, state, and federal taxes.

"Better than Grafskoy," Al's dad said, remembering his old hometown in Russia. He *really* loved it here.

Morris Winnikoff had a wonderful friend by the name of Morris Glass. The two Morrises had come over from Russia in 1925, pressed pants in the same dry cleaning establishment, and let their kids play together. Al Winnikoff and Irving Glass were born in the same year. When the boys were twenty-six years old, Morris Winnikoff was ready to retire from the laundry business. He *begged* Morris Glass to buy the La Tijera Washette, because he knew it would be a great investment for his friend.

No sale.

While Morris Glass and his son Irving continued to look for a business to buy, they just went on pressing pants and making a living in the old, uncomplicated way.

After the laundry was sold to someone else, the senior Winnikoff bought an income-producing property and sort of retired.

The younger Winnikoff went on to buy well-chosen properties in Malibu—one a year for twenty-five years, according to plan. He did his homework and started out with the cheapest stuff he could find: forty acres for $300 per acre. After all, now working for Douglas Aircraft as a technical writer, he was rich—making $90 per week, plus overtime, which he thought was like getting free money.

On the downside, he didn't like working for someone else. But on the upside there were plusses. The first was two great bosses—really great guys who taught him the business. The second was that he made about $15 more per week than he did in the laundry business. So he saved $15 a week, and a year later had another $780 to invest.

Twenty years later, in 1976, when all the men met again at a family reunion, Morris and Irving Glass were still looking for a business to buy. And still pressing pants for the other guy.

Morris Winnikoff, an uneducated foreigner, said to his educated, literate son, "Al, in morality and in business, it's much better to try to do something good and fail than to do nothing and succeed."

Even more pointed, he taught his son, "If you're going to do something, start now."

> **If you're going to do something, start now.**

The son took the father's advice and it never failed him.

Al gets a little misty-eyed and nostalgic when he talks about his dad, a man loved by one and all. Morris Winnikoff never once in his entire life brought shame or sorrow or grief or suffering to his family or friends. Or his customers. His family never once saw him drunk or in jail. He never cheated anyone. His children never went hungry or homeless and his wife knew she was secure with a good, solid, trustworthy, and faithful man. So she nagged him.

By the way, we didn't tell you the previous story so that you would run out and buy the nearest laundry as an investment, though if you feel this is a good move, then go for it. But following the investment advice we will lay out for you in this book actually involves taking a much smaller initial risk than the $25,000 asking price of the Winnikoffs' laundry—although saving even as little as $15 a week from your paycheck (which is how Al started when he went from $75 a week at the laundry to $90 a week at Douglas) might seem just as daunting to you now as buying that laundry had seemed to Morris Glass.

You might end up procrastinating. And if you procrastinate, you'll end up just as broke or scared twenty-five years from now as you are today. We don't want that to happen to you.

So start now. Start now and these authors will be very proud of you. Very proud indeed.

The Twelvefold Path to Millionairedom

Success in any endeavor requires concentration and single-minded attention to detail.

Willie Sutton, bank robber

As we said before, one of us, Al Winnikoff, has done very well for himself in real estate but has never owned a stock. So what makes him an expert on the type of investments we're going to talk about in this book?

That's where I come in. I'm Wayne Wagner. I'm the guy Al came to for the answer to the Philip Morris question: What would you be worth if you bought Philip Morris stock instead of (or in addition to) smoking? The answer to that question is what we referred to earlier as our inspiration to write this book.

What Al has done in the chapters so far is to lay out the most important lesson of all: If you don't save, nothing else matters. If you're going to invest, you need money set aside to invest with. If you're trying to get rich quick, forget about it. If you really get Al's message, the rest is easy.

My job is to make it easy for you to *do* the investing—and to make it totally effective in building toward your goal. Since there are so many ways to invest, a large part of my job is to discard a lot of interesting options. A whole lot.

In the next few chapters we'll go over a truly simple way of investing with a reasonable-risk, reasonable-return strategy. It doesn't take brilliance and it doesn't require a lot of hard work. And it doesn't require that you thread your way through thousands of confusing if not downright scary financial alternatives.

While I can think of a lot of ways to earn money faster, and certainly you've heard plenty of get-rich-quick strategies, this is the easiest, most sure-fire way. It's the way I invest myself. It's what I tell my family members to do (if they ask).

It's based on twelve simple concepts:

1. Save
2. Start now
3. Be patient
4. Take risk
5. Put the odds in your favor
6. Invest
7. Diversify
8. Keep your money working
9. Avoid costs at all costs
10. Avoid taxes
11. Never sell
12. Don't talk to anyone about your investing

Each of these is easier to understand than it may seem now. You'll see.

Let's get started with the first concept on our list.

Step 1: Save

Any society that saves will eventually become rich.

Hunter Lewis, author

You've heard Al's message on this. If you're still reading, it must make some sense to you, so I won't repeat it. But if you don't get the message, don't read any further. This book's not for you. Go have some fun. Hock your house up to 125 percent of the value, tap your 401(k) funds, run up your credit cards, and lease a fancy car. Enjoy.

By the way, did your bank ever tell you how long it will be until you pay off your credit card balance by paying the monthly minimum? Up to thirty years— *thirty;* no typo.

> **Let's get back to saving, which you should be doing regardless of how much debt you've run up on your credit cards.**

But let's get back to saving, which you should be doing regardless of how much debt you've run up on your credit cards.

It's easier to commit to saving if you have a clear goal of what you're saving for. Here are some thoughts that might trigger some motivation for you:

- So your children don't have to live hand-to-mouth like you did.
- To open your own business.
- So your retirement is more comfortable.
- So you can make a truly significant gift to your favorite charity.

- Because you're afraid Social Security won't be there when you need it.
- For a rainy day.
- Just in case.
- Because you have a peculiar affection for numbers with lots of zeros in them.
- Whatever motivates you to think beyond "I want it all, and I want it now."
- So you can walk up to your boss, look him straight in the eye, shake his hand, and say, "So long, Joe. I quit."

Unless you were extremely fortunate in your choice of ancestors, you'll just have to make another choice—between saving and becoming wealthy over the long term or, as we said at the beginning of this chapter, mortgaging your house, tapping your 401(k), and running up your credit cards so that you can pretend you're wealthy now. Despite what those flashy credit card ads would have you believe, you can't have it both ways. You must choose.

Now, if you're like most people, you don't even realize that you're *making* a choice. Most people don't choose to not save, they just believe that saving is impossible for them. If you're like them, you're now saying, "But I have no money left over to save with!" Baloney! You do, you can, and you will.

The sad, sad truth for the others is that average Americans spend every nickel they can get their hands on. They spend everything they earn and everything they can borrow. But becoming a millionaire is not an average outcome. Most Americans never become millionaires. They believe they can't, and they're dead right. Like a dachshund in a greyhound race, they just aren't built for it.

We have no advice for those people. If you're one of them, put this book down. However, if you're one of the people who wants to do it, has the guts to do it, but just doesn't know how . . . we can guide you.

We've said it over and over: nothing happens until you start your lifelong program of saving. Saving starts with not spending, and the best way to not spend is to never see the money. Here are some tips on how to get started:

- Take it out of your paycheck first, automatically.
- If you get a raise, put that away before you get used to spending it.
- If you get some unexpected money, start with that. Don't use the tax refund to pay down your credit card bill; you'll just run it up again. Don't use the inheritance from Aunt Eleanor to recarpet; it'll just wear out. Put it aside for yourself and your future.
- The most important thing is to start—and start now. If you can't save 10 percent of your income, start with 5 percent. If you can't save $100, save $50. But start! Get the habit! Start now!
- You can actually reduce the amount you drizzle away each and every month, and save it instead.

Spending and saving are not only opposites but they're also entirely different directions. When you spend, the money disappears. Poof—it's gone. Most of the time you can't even remember what bauble it was that amused you that day or that year.

When you save, the money grows. It begins saving for you faster and faster. And when you save, you become an entirely different person. You walk straighter, smile more, and catch fewer colds. Life starts working for you. It's no longer a constant battle against debt and depression. You become an investor, on your way to becoming a millionaire. Isn't that where you'd rather be down the road?

You can end up very, very unhappy if you make the wrong choice. According to the *New York Times*,[2] the average American homeowner who retires today has a nest egg of $115,000. Now compare this to the average net worth of the retiring nonhomeowner. He or she retires with—brace yourself—$800 of net worth. *Eight hundred dollars.* Imagine trying to live to age eighty-five on that! (Actually you might not have to worry—the less money you retire with, the shorter your life expectancy, according to the *Times*.)

Of course, when we speak of millionaires we are talking about the balance sheet and not a glitzy lifestyle. One of the first people who saw this book worried, "I wouldn't know *how* to live like a millionaire."

She needn't worry. If this program appeals to her and she has the self-assurance to use her money on what she values, she will not care about showing off to others. Most self-made millionaires do not flaunt their wealth.

[2] "A Growing Gap Between the Savers and the Save Nots," David Cy Johnson, *New York Times,* March 21, 1999.

Step 2: Start Now

Persistence is the first, and only, test of commitment.

Wayne Wagner, author

There are millions of reasons why you don't want to start now—the market's at an all-time high, you need a washing machine, life will come to an end if you don't own a new SUV, and so on.

Take my advice. Please. Start with a dollar if you can't do better. Good grief, how many ways are there to say this? Invest *now.*

Here's where we get into the numbers. If you want a million dollars at some point in the future, how much do you have to save per month?

We'll justify this later but, for now, accept that you can average a 10 percent return per year, which doubles your money every seven years. The following chart and graph clearly illustrate how much you need to save to reach millionairedom:

Current Age	Years to a Million Dollars at Age 65	Monthly Investment Required	Daily Investment Required
25	40	$179	$5.97
30	35	292	9.73
35	30	481	16.03
40	25	805	28.63
45	20	1382	46.07
50	15	2491	83.03

Wow, those numbers build up fast! If you're twenty-five and want a million dollars by age sixty-five, you need to put aside only $179 per month or $5.97 per day. If you fool around until you're fifty, you're going to have to shell out a lot! Or reduce your target.

Monthly Investment Required to Become a Millionaire by Age 65

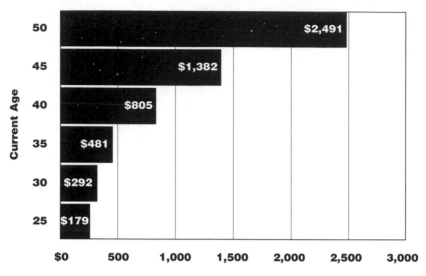

Now don't go crazy and tell me that you're forty-seven years old and can't turn back the clock. There's still a very good chance that you'll live at least another twenty-five years. And if you do, you're going to need money then. Probably more than you need it now. So if you invest $805 per month, you can be a millionaire by age seventy-two. That's better than dying broke or living out your years in the county home.

On the other hand, $179 a month is just $5.97 a day. You can probably save that by bagging your lunch or, as Al already showed, by kicking the smoking habit. You don't have to take a vow of poverty if you start soon enough.

And, incredible as it may seem, if you are *truly* concerned about the future welfare of a newborn child today, you need only start an investment program that requires $27 per month for your child to be a millionaire by age sixty. That's less than $1.00 per day!

Current Age	Years to a Million Dollars at Age 65	Monthly Investment Required	Daily Investment Required
5	60	$27	$.90
10	55	43	1.43
15	50	68	2.27
20	45	111	3.70
25	40	179	5.97

Monthly Investment Required to Become a Millionaire by Age 65

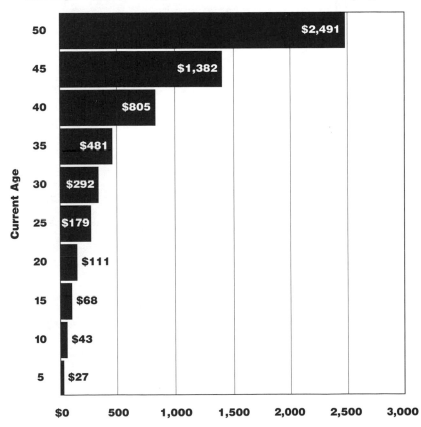

Albert Einstein, smart man, said that compound interest was the greatest invention of mankind. Now you see why!

Okay, it's time to get going! Here's what you need to do:

- Pay yourself first. Before you spend it on anything else, put it aside. The easiest way is to make it automatic.
- You'll want your bank to make an automatic transfer to your investment account (out of sight, out of mind).

On the following pages is a sample that shows you the simplicity of filling out one of these forms.

Vanguard U.S. Stock Index Funds
Account Registration Form

WBA7-197

 THE **Vanguard** GROUP

This form may not be used to open a brokerage account, individual retirement account (IRA), 403(b)(7), or any other Vanguard retirement plan. Visit us online at **www.vanguard.com** or call us to obtain the correct brokerage or retirement account form. Please refer to the enclosed instructions when completing this form.

If you need assistance, call us toll-free: **1-800-662-7447**. Please return your completed form in the enclosed business reply envelope or mail the form to **The Vanguard Group, P.O. Box 2600, Valley Forge, PA 19482-2600**. Please print in capital letters, preferably in black ink.

1. Account Information

Do you have other Vanguard accounts?   Yes   ✓ No

Please select *one* account type (A, B, C, or D) and provide the information requested for that section.

A. Individual, Joint,* or Attorney-in-Fact Account** *(One must be of legal age, for the state in which he/she resides, in order to be listed as an Individual or a Joint Owner of an account.)*

John Saver   0 1 / 0 1 / 1 9 7 0   1 2 3 4 5 6 7 8 9

Owner or Attorney-in-Fact (Agent)   Birth Date *(Month, Day, Year)*   Social Security Number
(First, Middle Initial [if used], Last)

Jennifer Saver   0 1 / 0 2 / 1 9 7 2   9 8 7 6 5 4 3 2 1

Joint Owner or Account Owner (Principal)   Birth Date *(Month, Day, Year)*   Social Security Number
(First, Middle Initial [if used], Last)

*Joint accounts will be registered as joint tenants with the right of survivorship unless you indicate otherwise on a separate, attached sheet.
**Attorney-in-Fact accounts will be registered in the Account Owner's (Principal's) Social Security number and must be accompanied by a Vanguard Power of Attorney Agreement.

B. Uniform Gifts/Transfers to Minors Act (UGMA/UTMA) Account*

Custodian's Name (One name only)   Birth Date *(Month, Day, Year)*   Social Security Number
(First, Middle Initial [if used], Last)

Minor's Name   Birth Date *(Month, Day, Year)*   Social Security Number
(First, Middle Initial [if used], Last)

This gift or transfer is being made under the   Uniform Gifts/Transfers to Minors Act.
Name of State
*UGMA/UTMA accounts will be registered in the minor's Social Security number.

C. Trust Account *(If all Trustees are not named below, please complete and attach a Vanguard Certificate of Authority form.)*

Trustee's Name *(First, Middle Initial [if used], Last)*   Co-Trustee's Name *(First, Middle Initial [if used], Last)*

Name of Trust Agreement   Name of Beneficiary

Trustee's Social Security or Employer Identification Number   Date of Trust Agreement *(Month, Day, Year)*

D. Business or Organization Account *(Additional documents may be needed before opening an account.)*

Name of Sole Proprietor or Names of Partners *(If applicable)*   Name of Business or Organization

Social Security Number *(For sole proprietor)*   Employer Identification Number *(For all other businesses/organizations)*

62 Millionaire

2. Address/Citizenship Information *(Please provide the requested information for the primary registrant only.)*

Address *(This information will be used as the address of record for all account mailings.)*

1 Millionaire Lane
Street Address and Apartment or Box Number

Saverstown   *P A*   *1 2 3 4 5*
City   State   Zip

9 9 9 5 5 5 5 5 5 5   *9 9 9 5 5 5 6 6 6 6*
Daytime Telephone Number   Evening Telephone Number

Citizenship *(Check one)*: ✓
      U.S. Citizen   Resident Alien   Nonresident Alien   Country of Residence *(For nonresident alien)*

3. Employment Information *(This section is optional.)*

Owner, Trustee, or Custodian

Occupation   Name of Employer

Employer's Street Address   City   State   Zip

    I am affiliated with or working for a member firm of the NASD.

Joint Owner or Co-Trustee

Occupation   Name of Employer

Employer's Street Address   City   State   Zip

    I am affiliated with or working for a member firm of the NASD.

4. Investment Information *(The minimum initial investment is $3,000 per fund or $1,000 for UGMA/UTMA accounts.)*

Fund Numbers	Fund Names	Amounts	
0 0 8 5	Total Stock Market Index Fund	$	
0 0 4 0	500 Index Fund	$	*3 0 0 0. 0 0*
0 0 9 8	Extended Market Index Fund	$	
0 8 5 9	Mid-Cap Index Fund	$	
0 0 4 8	Small-Cap Index Fund	$	
0 0 0 6	Value Index Fund	$	
0 8 6 0	Small-Cap Value Index Fund	$	
0 0 0 9	Growth Index Fund	$	
0 8 6 1	Small-Cap Growth Index Fund	$	
	TOTAL	$	

5. Method of Payment *(Please select only one [A, B, or C].)*

✓ **A.** My check(s) payable to *The Vanguard Group* is/are enclosed.

B. Please exchange $ from my identically registered account:

Fund Number   Account Number

C. Payment has previously been made by *(Select one)*   Phone exchange   Wire

      from

Date *(Month, Day, Year)*   Fund Number   Account Number *(Previously assigned)*

6. Vanguard Fund Express® Account Options *(Please refer to instructions for option descriptions.)*

> AIP — Automatic Investment Plan; minimum $50, maximum $100,000.
> AWP — Automatic Withdrawal Plan; minimum $50, maximum $100,000.

Bank Information *(Required for all Vanguard Fund Express and Vanguard Dividend Express™ options.)*

Saversbank   *555 555 5555*
Bank Name   Bank Telephone Number

Your Bank Account Type *(Check one)*:   Checking   Statement Savings   *(Sets up Automatic Transfer!)*

Selected Options

A. *0 0 4 0*   *500 Index Fund*   AIP   AWP
Fund Number   Fund Name

      $
Start Date *(M, D)*   Amount   ✓ Monthly   Every Other   Quarterly   Semiannually   Annually
                   Month

B.   AIP   AWP
Fund Number   Fund Name

      $
Start Date *(M, D)*   Amount   Monthly   Every Other   Quarterly   Semiannually   Annually
                   Month

Note: If no investment or withdrawal schedule is indicated for AIP or AWP, assets will be transferred on a monthly basis.

J. A. Sample
123 Street
Anywhere, USA 12345   1563

PAY TO THE
ORDER OF   *Tape Your Voided Check or Preprinted Deposit Slip Here. We cannot establish these options without it. (Please do not use staples.)*

                               Dollars

FOR: VOID

1:23456789:0123456789012"   1563

(over, please)

7. Distribution Options for Dividends and Capital Gains *(Please see instructions and check one option each for dividend and capital gains distributions for each fund you selected in Section 4.)*

Unless a box is checked, all distributions will be reinvested in additional shares.

Distribution	Reinvest in Shares	Transfer to Bank Via Dividend Express*	Send Check
Dividends		X (Important!)	
Capital Gains		X	

*Please provide bank information and a voided check or preprinted deposit slip as described in Section 6.

8. Signatures of All Account Owners *(Please read carefully and sign below exactly as registered in Section 1.)*

- I/We have full authority and legal capacity to purchase fund shares.
- I/We have received a current prospectus of the funds and agree to be bound by its terms.
- If I/we have chosen a Fund Express option, I/we authorize Vanguard, upon telephonic request, to pay amounts representing redemption(s) made by me/us or to secure payment of amounts invested by me/us by initiating credit or debit entries to my/our account at the bank named in Section 6. I/We authorize the bank to accept any such credits or debits to my/our account without responsibility for the correctness thereof. I/We further agree Vanguard will not be liable for any loss, liability, cost, or expense for acting upon my/our telephonic request. It is understood that this authorization may be terminated by me/us at any time by written notification to Vanguard and to the bank. The termination request will be effective as soon as Vanguard has had a reasonable amount of time to act upon it.
- **Under penalty of perjury, I/we also certify that:**
  a. The number shown on this form is my/our correct taxpayer identification number(s).
  b. I am/We are not subject to backup withholding because (i) I/we have not been notified by the Internal Revenue Service that I am/ we are subject to backup withholding as a result of a failure to report all interest or dividends, or (ii) the IRS has notified me/us that I am/we are no longer subject to backup withholding. *Note:* **Cross out item "b" if you have been notified by the IRS that you are subject to backup withholding because of underreporting interest or dividends on your tax return.**

The Internal Revenue Service does not require your consent to any provision of this document other than the certifications required to avoid backup withholding.

Please sign here. *(If joint account, all owners must sign. Please attach additional sheet if necessary.)*

X

Signature *(Account Owner, Trustee, Attorney-in-Fact, Partner, Custodian, etc.)*   Date *(Month, Day, Year)*

X

Signature *(Joint Account Owner, Co-Trustee, Attorney-in-Fact, Partner, etc.)*   Date *(Month, Day, Year)*

Please check this box if you would like to receive an information kit, including an application, for Vanguard Direct Deposit Service™. This service lets you invest your paycheck, Social Security check, or other U.S. government payment directly into your Vanguard account(s). Note: Deposits must be for $100 or more.

Still Feeling Hopeless?

Okay, try this:

1. Make a budget. See exactly where your money comes from and where it goes over the course of a year. Find something you can cut back on.
2. Sign a contract, the one on the previous page. Make a written goal for your monthly savings—$100, $250—whatever you feel you can afford ($26, $13, $5.37. . .).
3. Put yourself on probation. Promise that for three months you will stick *precisely* to your plan. Trust us, you won't even miss the money you'll be saving.
4. After one year, and after every raise, increase the amount you save by 10 percent. If you're now saving $10, move it up to $11; if you're saving $100, raise it to $110.

    This is really the most important part. Why? *Because if you increase the amount you save the minute you get a raise, you'll be putting that extra money out of sight—where it can safely earn interest—before it ever goes into your pocket. And if it's never been in your pocket, taking it away will never feel like a deprivation.* But don't try to save *all* of your raise; you need some consumption to balance your life now as well as in the future. Saving *most* of your raise, however, is one of the easiest ways to significantly increase the amount of your savings.
5. Never, *ever* abandon this plan. If you do, you'll ruin everything. Remember, you made *three* contracts: a contract with these authors, the one you signed and sent to your fund management company, and the one you made with yourself to stay on the path to millionairedom.

Step 3: Be Patient

It is precisely because most people are not willing to subordinate their interests to those of future generations, that human societies throughout history have been so mired in poverty.

                                                        Hunter Lewis, author

A man asks God, "God, what is a million years like to you?"

God answers, "A million years to me is like a second is to you."

The man asks, "God, what is a million dollars like to you?"

God answers, "A million dollars to me is like a penny is to you."

The man asks, "God, will you give me a penny?"

God answers, "Sure—just give me a second."

Such is the power of compound interest.

Actually this God is being pretty stingy. If you do the math, God is paying interest at the rate of 0.001842 percent per year. At this rate, if you invested $10,000 for a year with the Bank of God, you'd make a whole eighteen cents in interest for the year.

However, at a more reasonable 10 percent per year return, it would take God only 194 years to turn a mere penny into a million dollars. Now a 194-year investment might not do you a lot of good personally, but you might want to consider a very small investment to set up a scholarship fund for your great-great-great-great-great-great-great-grandchildren.

Regardless of how it's done in heaven, Albert Einstein was right—compound interest is truly the greatest invention on the earthly plane. But it takes time to work its magic.

So the strategy we suggest here is a *very* long-term one. It requires that you stay with it year by year, decade by decade. We call this the "tortoise" strategy. We just plod along, year after year, while the magic keeps on working.

Let me give you an idea of what I mean by the long term. After I graduated from college, my family moved to a small town in northern Wisconsin called Antigo, population around seven thousand. There are a lot more millionaire potato farmers than there are millionaire investors in Antigo (and probably not too many of either).

My younger brother still lives there. He has two beautiful daughters, Kim and Allison, ages seventeen and fifteen. They're good students, and they both work after school and on weekends at McDonald's. Minimum wage. And guess where they put some of that money? In a Roth IRA!

What? You can't understand how two teenaged girls could be thinking about a retirement account? Maybe it's the fresh country air. Or maybe they read this book! (More likely their father did.)

In case you don't know what a Roth IRA is, it's a way to set aside earnings for a tax-free-accumulation Individual Retirement Account. Let's take a minute to talk about IRAs, Roth IRAs, and employee-sponsored 401(k) plans. If you're serious about becoming a millionaire, you need to bone up on what these plans can do for you. Take our word for it, the tax advantages can really accelerate the growth of your funds.

IRA (Individual Retirement Account)

Congress created these so that individuals can set aside personal money for retirement *before taxes are taken out!* The tax savings is the important part. If you had $100 that you wanted to invest, you'd have only $70 left if you paid taxes at a 30 percent rate.

Clearly, you're going to get to a million faster by saving hundred-dollar bills than by saving seventy-dollar bills. When you withdraw these retirement savings, however, you will pay ordinary income taxes on the money you made. If you're self-employed or if your employer doesn't have a pension plan for you, you must set up an IRA.

Roth IRA

A Roth IRA is similar, but you get the option of paying the taxes at the start, then paying *no* taxes when you withdraw. This can be an important advantage over the long term, particularly for the kind of ongoing investment plan we recommend here. Basically, you can pay the tax on a little money now, instead of on a lot of accumulated gain later.

401(k)

Many employers sponsor a plan called a 401(k) which allows your employer and/or you to contribute tax-deferred funds for your retirement. If you leave your employer, you usually have the option to transfer your earned retirement funds and savings into your new employer's 401(k) or into your own IRA. Be sure to do this—if the funds are not transferred within sixty days, you will not only have to pay the tax on them, but spending these funds will also destroy all the good work you've done to date.

SEP (Simplified Employee Pension) or Keogh Plans

These allow individuals who are self-employed to create tax-sheltered retirement accounts. While detailed analysis of the pros and cons of each of these alternatives is well beyond the scope of this book, the Internet provides a wealth of information on these types of investments. One place to start is invest-faq.com. You can also find many other interesting sites through your favorite search engine.

While my nieces deserve credit for thinking ahead at such a young age, I would caution them not to get obsessed with their savings plans. Frankly, I could never stick to a program that I felt was denying me the joy of living today, and I wouldn't encourage Allison and Kim to live that way either.

The only way you're going to be able to stick with a process whose payoff is a long way into the future is to enjoy yourself along the way—which means that you have to keep some balance in your life. Don't be a miser! You won't like what it turns you into, and very likely the people around you won't like it either. We want you committed to the program, not to an asylum.

Whatever you enjoy, enjoy it to its fullest. Enjoy music, skydive, cruise the Internet, whatever pleases you. My passion happens to be bicycling, and my custom bike gives me great pleasure whether I'm riding it or just looking at it. Please make sure you do whatever you do to please yourself, not to show off. Showing off *and* becoming an investor never worked for us, never worked for Charley Spenditall, and it won't work for you either.

And remember, while you're out there enjoying life, your tortoise investment will be faithfully doing its work for you and growing bigger every year. Still not sure that the way of the tortoise is for you? Consider this: According to Collier's Encyclopedia, the giant tortoise lives longer than any other animal.

Step 4: Take Risk

You don't have a chance if you don't take a chance.

Author unknown

In the table on page 57, we worked out the required savings numbers for a 10 percent interest rate. If you've been to a bank lately you know they aren't paying 10 percent on savings accounts. They're paying something far less than half that amount. And that's not going to cut it for you.

. . . you know they aren't paying 10 percent on savings accounts.

The table below is the same as the one on page 57, except we've added a column of the monthly investment required to accumulate a million dollars at a 5 percent interest rate.

Current Age	Years to a Million Dollars at Age 65	Monthly Investment Required at 10%	Monthly Investment Required at 5%
25	40	$179	$672
30	35	292	899
35	30	481	1222
40	25	805	1701
45	20	1382	2455
50	15	2491	3761

Big numbers, right? To tell the truth, it's just too hard to become a millionaire at a 5 percent return. We're going to have to find something more productive to do with your money.

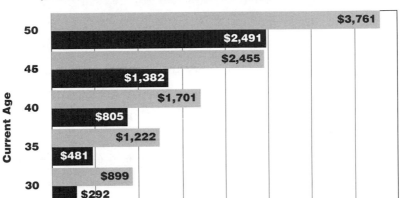

Monthly Investment Required
(Shaded bars at 5% interest; black bars at 10% interest)

This isn't a something-for-nothing world, so you'll have to give something up to get the returns you need. You'll have to give up that comforting certain return, where your assets gain in value a little bit every day.

In fact, you're going to have to put your money in a place where the value will go up and down, sometimes by significant amounts. This fluctuating value is what economists call *risk*. Risk sounds like a bad thing, like something you would want to avoid. But we have two pieces of good news for you.

First, you get paid for taking on this risk. Nobody would own these up-and-down assets unless they got some extra reward— the reward is a higher return over the long term.

Second, the assets go up and down, but they go up twice as often as they go down! So, for a long-term investor, *these daily ups and downs are irrelevant.* We're interested in the forest, not the trees. We're betting on the beautiful trend, not the ugly zits, blips, and wobbles. We're betting on the overall climate, not the daily weather.

One more thought: *Risk is everywhere.* You can't avoid risk by hiding your head in the sand. If you took your $179 each month and hid it in the basement, it would be worth only $85,920 in forty years—far short of the million. The very real risks in this scenario would be the painful consequences you might have to endure later in life. Even if you get only halfway to your goal, it's still over five times better than hoarding!

Okay, so what if you had invested this $85,920 as a lump-sum contribution and earned the 11.2 percent average large-stock return? How long would it take for that sum to turn into a million dollars? The answer: twenty-three years, three months— less time than it would take you to accumulate a million by saving $805 per month. Such is the power of long-term investing, especially if front-loaded with a big initial investment.

My father-in-law was suspicious to the point of paranoia. When gold was selling for $800 an ounce, he convinced himself that The End of Life as We Know It was upon us and the only safe investment was gold coins. Rather than put it in a bank, he buried it like a pirate. (Don't bother looking; he moved it before he passed away.)

What's gold worth at the turn of the millennium? Less than $300 an ounce. He lost five dollars out of every eight he saved—a return of negative 62.5 percent!

There is no twenty-year period in U.S. history where stocks depreciated 62.5 percent. The safest thing he could think of— gold secretly buried in the compost heap—was, in fact, about the riskiest storehouse imaginable for his money (other than

carrying it in a sack into a grubby waterfront bar, of course).
Imagine how rich his children would be if he had followed
the advice in this book through the '80s and the '90s.

There's another important lesson here in my father-in-law's
story. He let himself be swayed by the depression of the moment;
he panicked in the face of trends he couldn't understand and
couldn't imagine reversing. It's the destiny of the pessimists to
miss out in the best of times. Remember the naysayers' mantra
of just a few years ago, "Our children will have fewer opportunities than we had"? Then came the communications/Internet
revolution. In truth the naysayers, whose pessimism my father-
in-law swallowed whole, knew nothing.

We suggest that you take systematic risk by participating fully
in the economy. Stay with the risk that the long-haul economy will remain robust and adaptive.

Offsetting *these* risks are the risks of retiring without enough
money to keep you from a bitter—and likely shortened—
retirement. And along the way you'll reduce the chance of
becoming a burden on your children or your community.

A million books have told you to put 60 percent of your
investments in stocks and 40 percent in bonds. We're not sticking with the common wisdom. Most of the books just repeat
something the author once heard but never questioned, like,
"You will cause your mother great bodily harm if you step on
the cracks."

The real difference is the long horizon, combined with a
clearheaded, determined, and aggressive goal. We want you to
become a millionaire on $179 monthly installments (refer
again to table on page 70).

The second rule is preserve the assets. The first rule is get some assets worth preserving. The time for caution is way down the road . . . not now.

Those same million books also tell you that the first step is to make an investment plan—how much you're going to need per month when you retire, how much you need now for living expenses, and on and on. Most people throw up their hands in frustration. We suggest a much simpler plan, one that anybody can understand. It can be stated in six words: *"I plan to become a millionaire."*

Still, something could happen that would shake all of us— you, Al, and me—to the bottom of our souls. Next Monday could bring disaster. What if stocks go down 40 percent in twenty-four hours? How about 80 percent? What if an asteroid hits the earth? Malibu slides into the ocean? World War III? Will it happen? Not likely, but never say never. If it were to happen, it would likely happen faster than you—or anybody—could react. When it was over we'd need to pick up what's left, pretend it never happened, pretend it won't happen again, and shuffle forward with (dampened) enthusiasm.

I plan to become a millionaire!

Therefore, save, save, save, invest, invest, invest. For those who do, the best is yet to come.

The only true solace is that, whatever happens, it's always better to have some money in your pocket than none.

STEP 5: Put the Odds in Your Favor

If someone offers to bet you that he can make the jack of spades jump out of the deck and spit cider in your ear, don't take that bet. You're going to end up with an earful of cider.

Bret Maverick, *from the television series* Maverick

I heard on the radio that over 50 percent of lottery tickets are sold to only 5 percent of the lottery players. We have an equation for people who repeatedly go for broke against enormous odds: G–R–E–E–D–Y + L–A–Z–Y = L–O–S–E–R.

Someone once called the lottery a tax on mathematical ineptitude. Indeed. Not only do the losers outnumber the winners millions to one, but *it also isn't even a fair game;* fair would be if the money paid out were close to the money paid in.

No chance. The state and the ticketsellers pocket one-half to two-thirds of the bet before letting the suckers fight over the scraps. Even Las Vegas would be ashamed at that level of scam.

Let's take a look at the actual payback you can expect from gambling and/or the state lottery versus investing in the stock market.

According to numbers quoted in various places on the Internet, every $100 "bet" pays back as follows:

- Craps $95 to $98
- Keno $78
- Roulette $94.74
- Sports $90
- Lottery $50
- Stock Market $110

The nature of gambling against the house is that the house wins more often than it loses, and the accumulated house gains are the shortfall between the take-in and the payout. Clearly, the state lottery skim is outrageously higher than anything the casinos take.

Of course, what we see on television is the happy lottery-winner-of-millions and not the millions of unhappy losers. Imagine *that* kind of interview on television:

INTERVIEWER: Ernest, I understand you didn't win the lottery today.

ERNEST: No, no luck today.

INTERVIEWER: Have you ever won?

ERNEST: No, but my uncle won five bucks in 1994.

INTERVIEWER: How often do you play?

ERNEST: Every time, twice a week. Thirty tickets. Been doing it for ten years.

INTERVIEWER: So you spend $60 per week on lottery tickets. How much do you make a week?

ERNEST: I make good money, about $300 a week.

INTERVIEWER: So you spend 20 percent of your income on lottery tickets! What does your wife think?

ERNEST: Faith, she enjoys it. We read the numbers together when they're announced. It gives us hope for a better life.

INTERVIEWER: You've spent $60 a week for ten years. I asked our financial expert how much money you'd have now if you'd invested that in an S&P 500 index fund instead of playing the lottery. He said that $60 a week, invested from January 1990 through December 1999, would be worth nearly $100,000. $98,331.12, to be precise. Instead you lost $60 times 52 weeks times 10 years, equals $31,200. Net difference: $129,531.12. That's almost $130,000! Wouldn't you be better off if you had invested the money?

ERNEST: Yes, but if I won I could have been a millionaire.

To tell the truth, we can't really understand what motivates lottery ticket buyers. The same amount of money, invested as we're laying out in this book, has an enormously higher expected payout over twenty-five years. But the something-for-nothing crowd always finds it more thrilling to beat the odds than to use the same money to systematically make themselves rich.

Not all gamblers are losers. There are a few professional gamblers who actually make a living at it. But not many.

On the other hand, the stock market, while often likened to gambling, actually has a wonderfully positive payoff as long as you stick to a low-cost, long-term plan. The 10 percent payoff is the payoff per year.

But here's the point: Gambling risk isn't the same as the investment risk we talked about in the previous chapter. The casinos in Las Vegas have a slight edge in *their* favor, and look what palaces they've built with their winnings. What we're laying out for you is an investment strategy in which risk has a slight edge in *your* favor. Play the game enough times and you're certain to come out a winner.

Step 6: Invest

The single biggest time-waster in the world is not completing what you start.

John Gardner, time management specialist

Investing is not the same as saving. Investing is not about collecting interest. Investing is owning productive assets.

As those produce goods and services, they create returns. Not only do you get a better return on what you invest, but you also earn returns on the returns you've already earned! These "Einsteinian compounding" returns make you a millionaire.

The easy way is to own a share of the production and hire someone to run it for you. This is known as owning stocks. The next table shows the benefit of investing in stocks from 1926 through 1998.[3]

Asset	Annual Return
Bank Interest (Treasury Bills)	3.8%
Bonds (30-year U.S. Treasury Bonds)	5.3%
Large-Company Stocks	11.2%

It was a great seventy-three years.

When my children were born I opened an account in each of their names for college funds. I put $250 a month into each

---

[3]Ibbotson Associates, Inc., as quoted in *Investment News,* April 19, 1999

account, automatically withdrawing the money from my checking account. I kept the funds invested in stocks. Eighteen years later, when my son, Eric, was admitted to Dartmouth College, there was over $83,000 in his account, even though we had stayed invested through some lean years in the market. Almost $30,000 of it was appreciation on the payments I made into the fund.

I used the money to pay four years' tuition in advance, the day he was accepted, which saved us an additional bundle. It couldn't have come at a better time, because at that point I was funding a business and didn't have any spare cash.

> **You earn returns on the returns you've already earned.**

Looks like we have a clear winner here: investing in stocks. But which stocks to own? How do you find the good stocks? In the dynamic American economy, products go out of style, factories get old, and keeping your money productive could take a lot of effort. Fortunately, there is an easy way.

You want to own stocks you will never sell. In other words, big companies with the strength and flexibility to remain productive for a period as long as your investment horizon. Sure, these companies will cycle in and out of special advantage, but to people with courage and patience (namely, our readers) those ups and downs are meaningless over long periods.

How do you pick those companies? There's a world of advice and opinion around, mostly offered by earnest men and women whose age is less than the number of years you intend to hold the assets. Worse, most of them make money only when you buy or sell, not when you invest. So their interests aren't the same as yours.

But you're in luck again. You don't have to pick the best stocks, you can be content with the average stocks. There's a very easy way to own the average stocks: *own all the stocks!*

That's what investing in an *index fund* does for you. But before we talk specifically about index funds, let's make sure you understand the other investment choices available to you.

The first thing we want to do is to assure you that you are smarter than you may think. If you've come to us overwhelmed, you have good reason to be. There are a horrific number of books, articles, advice sheets, pamphlets, and brochures out there that are spewing out investment information faster than any human being can possibly read them, let alone understand them. So just because you may not understand each and every word and concept we throw at you right this second, remember that by the time you reach the end of this book you will understand *everything.* Take heart that 99 percent of the world's millionaires are not geniuses. And 99 percent of the world's geniuses are not millionaires! Forget the billionaires and overnight Internet wizards and how they made fortunes. We ordinary folks can't do that. That's why we're going to make our advice simple.

Everyone these days, from the experts on TV to the guy at the checkout counter in your supermarket, is giving you investment advice. But what exactly is an investment? It's something worth money that you buy and hold for a time in the hopes that you get more from it than you paid. The 1998 Ford you drive to work every day isn't an investment. It's a consumable, something you use up as you go along. Consumption is the opposite of investment.

One important difference between consumption and investment is that an investment, if it grows in value, allows you to
consume more later than if you had consumed it all right now.

The simplest kind of investment is *savings.* You could bury
some money in a coffee can, but that wouldn't be an investment
because it wouldn't grow anything but mold. If you put it into a
savings account or a *U.S. government bond,* it would be an investment because you would have more after you'd held it for a while.

Buying Corporate Bonds

Instead of investing in a bank or the government, you could
invest in the bonds of a company *(corporate bonds).* Investing in a
bond fund is like lending money to a corporation (or, in the case
of government bonds, lending money to the government). The
corporation that issues the bonds must pay you back at a fixed rate
of interest, quarterly or annually. Because there is always a chance
that any company could run into financial trouble—which would
mean it would be unable to pay back the bonds—you get a higher
rate of interest as an enticement to take on that little bit of risk.

Buying Individual Shares of Stock

But not all investors own bonds in corporations. Some hold
shares in the company, usually called *stock.* What's the difference
between bonds and stock? With bonds, you collect your interest
and get your money back at the end. With a stock, you don't have
a guarantee. What you get is your share (this is why they're called
shares) of the profit after the expenses and after the bondhold-
ers have been paid what's due them. Unlike a bond's fixed rate
of return on your investment, a stock's rate of return fluctuates
with the company's profits and losses.

Since there's no guarantee on shares of stock, they are a lot riskier than bonds. They may pay a dividend, which is like interest on a bond but usually much less than what a bondholder gets. What makes a stock attractive is that it will rise in value if the company becomes more valuable. This is called *capital appreciation* and results when the price of the stock rises.

Even the government works to encourage people to own stocks. The tax bite on capital appreciation is less than the tax on interest or dividends, because the government recognizes that stock is necessary to build the companies that add to the nation's wealth.

Most investors, except those who own a company or whose employer encourages them to buy company stock, typically own more than one stock. Why? Because this bunch of stocks, often called a portfolio, is less risky than piling all your money into only one company's stock. One company may fail but it's unlikely that all would fail at the same time.

This principle of reducing your risk by buying lots of different stocks is called *diversification*. It is the subject of the next chapter.

Investing in Mutual Funds

At the beginning of the twentieth century, some bright people got the idea that they could help investors, who are usually busy earning a living, do a better job of deciding what stocks to hold in a portfolio. So they gathered together a bundle of stocks that *they* thought were good and sold shares in the bundle. This bundle of stocks is called a *mutual fund*.

The first mutual fund was the Massachusetts Investment Trust, which was established in 1924. The object of the fund was to give safety through diversity to small-time investors so they would not get clobbered in a down-market such as the Big One from 1929 to 1939. (That's when we had 24 percent unemployment in the U.S.)

The people who manage mutual funds charge a fee for watching over the bundle of stocks, occasionally pushing one or two out and replacing them with something more attractive. The idea is that investors would be better off relying on the mutual fund manager's financial expertise than they would be on their own.

Only it doesn't always work that way. In fact, as we will discuss in great detail, many mutual fund managers have had trouble generating returns for their clients in excess of what the stock market was doing as a whole.

While only a handful of mutual funds were in business in 1930, there are over seven thousand today. Some of them have never shown a profit. Many of them have substantial gains one year and disaster the next. While mutual fund managers are picked for their brilliance and are among the best financial minds in the world, they are only human. Like any ordinary mortal, they cannot consistently predict what the stock market will do and they cannot call the perfect shots every single year. No one can.

How to solve this dilemma? You won't find the answer in your mutual fund manager's crystal ball, but you will find it in the next Step.

Step 7: Diversify

In this business there are fifty ways to foul up. If you're a genius, you can think of twenty-five of them. And you ain't no genius.

From the movie Body Heat

Up and down, up and down—the market's precise daily movements are impossible to predict or avoid.

But within the tide there are subcurrents: one stock rises while another declines. How do you pick which stock to own or which mutual fund to invest in? The truth is, even the experts find it tough to pick the right stocks most of the time. *You don't have a chance.* So what do you do?

Make the subcurrents work for you! Offset the stocks going down with the stocks going up. That way your portfolio doesn't suffer, because over time twice as many stocks go up as go down.

Holding lots and lots of stocks is a good idea because it keeps you from loading up on what could turn out to be a very bad stock. That's what diversification is all about.

Carried to the logical extreme, you as an individual could buy and then hold all stocks! Absurd? Not really. Because there *are* funds that do hold all stocks, or at least a very broad assortment of stocks. They're called *index funds.*

To fully understand what an index fund is, we need to reintroduce the concept of the *stock market index.* Stock market indexes were created to help investors answer the question "What did the market do today?" An index, then, is a group of stocks whose collective price movement is thought to measure "the market."

This is what radio and TV newscasters are always referring to when you hear them talking about how many points "the

Dow Jones industrial average" went up or down on a given day. Historically, the Dow Jones industrial average, an index of thirty important industrial companies, has been accepted as the best barometer of what's happening in the stock market on a minute-by-minute basis. In recent years the NASDAQ 100 index has become an important indicator of the performance of the technology sector of the market, which seems to chart its own path independent of the Dow Jones selection of thirty companies.

Even so, both the Dow Jones and NASDAQ indexes are narrowly based on a smallish number of issues and can hardly be said to represent all stocks. At the other extreme is the Wilshire 5000 index, which contains every single publicly owned stock, now over seven thousand companies. (It's called the Wilshire "5000" because when the index was created there were only five thousand publicly traded companies on the stock market.) But because some of the companies in the Wilshire 5000 index are hardly ever traded, a more convenient index is the Standard & Poor's 500 stock index, which is comprised of five hundred stocks designed to represent the whole economy.

From these indexes—these indicators of the overall performance of the stock market—was born the index fund, the investment that will be the centerpiece of your path to millionairedom.

Index Funds

Index funds give you tons of diversification, as much as you can get anywhere. You can buy index funds that mimic the Dow Jones average, the Wilshire 5000 index, even international funds. The Web site indexfunds.com lists over 180 different index funds, and they didn't find them all.

All these have advantages, but the most well-known and readily available are the funds that mimic the S&P 500 index of five hundred large stocks. Because the S&P 500 index is thought to be most representative of the economy as a whole, it is used as the basis for most of the more popular index funds. The S&P 500 index is published in most newspapers, so you could look in the financial section to see how your investment performed every day. As you will see later, in Step 11, there are very good reasons why we recommend that you shouldn't do this.

Early in my career, I was fortunate to play a part in the birth of the index fund. Okay, I'm partial. Maybe even biased. But even if I weren't biased, the evidence is increasingly hard to refute.

Year	Percentage of Mutual Funds Outperformed by the Index Funds
1999	53
1998	85
1997	91
1996	75
1995	84
1994	78
1993	34
1992	42
1991	43
1990	65
1989	78
1988	49
1987	61
1986	64
1985	72
1984	72
1983	64
1982	49
1981	29
1980	57

Here's how to read the table above: The first line says that in 1999 the index funds outperformed 53 percent of all mutual funds. The best record for index funds was in 1997, when they beat 91 percent, and the worst year was 1981, when the index fund performance beat only 29 percent of all mutual funds.

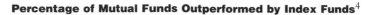

Percentage of Mutual Funds Outperformed by Index Funds[4]

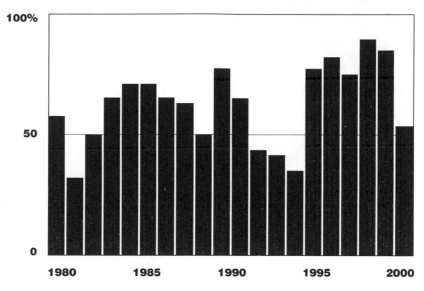

The above illustration shows the same data as the table on page 86: a bar above the 50 percent mark shows that the index funds outperformed more than half of the mutual funds. Recent years, up to 1999, have been particularly strong for index funds.

Because there are only a handful of index funds among the thousands of mutual funds, the bulk of mutual funds are actively managed: the mutual fund managers pick stocks that they believe will outperform the index and help them beat the market. Clearly, they haven't succeeded. The score since 1980:

Active Mutual Funds Win	**Index Funds Win**
6 years out of 20	14 years out of 20

---

[4]For year 2000 figures, see our Web site at www.lunchmoneymillionaire.com.

Get the message? These index funds, which don't even *try* to pick good stocks, outperform most of the mutual funds that engage in stock picking. Although the extreme overperformance we saw in the 1990s won't last forever, there are good reasons why the index funds are competitive in performance. In a couple of chapters, we'll tell you the built-in advantages that help the index funds perform well.

Index funds, however, will never, ever match the number-one best performing mutual fund of the quarter. Or, for that matter, for longer periods such as a year or even five years. So why would you not buy the hot-performing mutual fund? Four reasons:

1. The past performance of mutual funds seems to have little to do with future performance. The top performer today is no more likely to be in the top 25 percent of all funds next period than any other fund. And, worse still, there are indications that mutual funds that perform poorly are likely to continue to perform poorly. Beauty is skin deep; ugly seems to go clear to the bone.

2. All this effort that mutual fund managers expend to beat the market turns out to be costly to investors. "You get what you pay for" seems to be an exception when it comes to mutual fund fees.

3. Most mutual fund managers focus on performing well every quarter. This short-term focus leads them to hyperactive buying and selling choices they would not make if their interests coincided with yours. The tortoise index fund, in contrast, has a very long horizon: it buys to hold forever.

4. When you try to pick the best mutual fund of the future you will, being human, tend to buy the best mutual fund

of the recent past. It will have had very high performance—
before you buy it. But what happens when that hot hand goes
cold after you buy it? You'll give up, sell the mutual fund, fork
over more than 20 percent of your gains (if any) to the tax
man, and force yourself to start all over again. This is great.
Great for Uncle Sam, great for brokers, great for mutual fund
managers, but not very great at all for your chances of financial success.

My daughter Wendy asked me to help her with the materials her company gave her on 401(k) choices. The information her company provides shows only one type of number:
historical rates of return.

Let's try an experiment. Which of the actual rates of return
provided to Wendy do you prefer?

5.37%   8.83%   13.84%   24.77%

Let me guess which one you picked. How about 24.77
percent? Cosmic! If you could invest your $179 at 24.77 per-
cent, you would end up with $68,407,703, not just a measly
million.

We are about to have an epidemic of woulda, coulda, shoulda
here. Why didn't they tell me *ahead* of time how lucky/smart
they were going to be? Better yet, why won't anybody tell me
who's going to return 24.77 percent over the *next* ten years?

Sorry, nobody can. The past number is not enough information to tell if the performance is repeatable.

In fact the market of the past will not repeat, nor would a
mutual fund manager's reaction to it. The numbers Wendy's company provides are most likely useless—misguided at best and mis-
leading at worst.

So let's look further at the alternative that has a chance of delivering accurate market performance: the index fund.

Besides good performance, index funds give you three big advantages:

1. They give you as much diversification as you can get anywhere, though others will argue that you should also invest in small companies, and in non-U.S. companies, and so on. I wouldn't disagree, but which index fund is not as important as getting started in some index fund. There's all the action you need in the simple, plodding, S&P 500 index fund. You can always expand into other types of investments later, as you accumulate assets and knowledge.
2. Because they are far easier to run than stock-picking mutual funds, the index funds' administration fees are much less.
3. Because index funds trade much less, they spend little for trading or for taxes on trading. Instead, they keep the assets working for *you*.

One quick story. When Vanguard first came out with their index fund, I was one of the first investors with my Individual Retirement Account (IRA). I wasn't account number 1, but I am account number 5591. (There are now over ten million accounts. When I call Vanguard and give them my account number, they ask "What's the rest of it?")

Well, back then, the index funds were sold through brokers. I walked up Wilshire Boulevard in Santa Monica to the Paine Webber office, which was sponsoring the fund. I asked the receptionist if I could see a representative and was escorted over to Gary. He was everything you would expect a stock salesman to be: tall, handsome, a good talker . . . and barely able to keep himself from drooling. When I told him what I wanted to invest in, his first reaction was one of great curiosity. What did I know that he might be able to sell to his other clients?

Curiosity quickly turned to horror when I told him I didn't want to try picking funds that would outperform; I'd be perfectly happy with an index fund that did average (an *average* index fund was better than the average of all mutual funds).

Gary stared at me. What I wanted was beyond comprehension. *All* investors wanted to beat the market; there wasn't any person who wasn't looking to outperform. I left him with an order and a "now I've seen everything" look on his face. I never saw him again, nor did I need to. He would only try to talk me out of my well-conceived strategy.

That was then, but it probably wouldn't be any different now. Don't expect a stockbroker to support you in this investment strategy. Stockbrokers work for commissions (called "load fees" for mutual funds) and they won't make any when you invest in index funds. And today they need that commission more than ever, what with all these computer-savvy people bypassing the broker and doing their trading directly on the Internet.

If, like my daughter, you are deciding on 401(k) choices offered by your employer and see that these choices do not offer an index fund, what should you do? There's not much you can do, actually, other than give the plan administrator a copy of this book. If none of your employer's choices is an obvious one, look for the investments with low administration fees, low turnover, and broad diversification.

Step 8: Keep Your Money Working

When times are good, people remember the good times.
When times are bad, people remember the bad times.

Source unknown

It's hard to watch the stock market for long without developing an impression that it doesn't seem to know where it wants to go.

Up, down . . . the experts and analysts always have a reason for what it did yesterday, but few can tell you with any precision what it will do tomorrow. Any person who could accurately predict financial market movements would own the world in ninety days.

Strip away everything else and the market reveals itself to be a barometer of . . . everything! All hopes and fears, all profits and losses, all government and private actions, all rolled up in one impenetrable ball. Your big bet is on the optimism and productivity of America (or, increasingly, the world). Many years ago, a wise friend called this "the risk of being alive." This is a bet you have to make no matter what course you choose.

We have seen many types of economic models in the past, some of which are still sputtering today. The religious economic models failed. The royal economic models failed. The mercantile economic models failed, as did the dictator models, the Marxist "people's paradise" models, the Japan, Inc. model, and the pad-the-Swiss-bank-account kleptocracy models. The only economic model that has consistently, for over two hundred years, given its citizens a high standard of living is the American economic model.

Why? Because it is based on a tremendous personal freedom found nowhere else in the world. It is not perfect, but nothing gives the American people a greater sense of security and attachment to their nation than home ownership, business ownership, and stock ownership. There is a tremendous paradox in America's low personal savings rate, because the total amount of overall American investment in inventions, factories, office buildings and schools is the highest in the world. It is that overall willingness to invest and believe in the future that makes us the most productive country on earth.

Because of this unheralded personal economic freedom, U.S. products and services are loved worldwide. Karl Marx and his theories cannot hold a candle to Walt Disney, Levi Strauss, Coca-Cola, and McDonald's. Fear not for the future of the U.S.A. The forces of freedom, open markets, and the constant discovery of new ways of doing things and making things that *customers want to buy* will keep us ahead of the pack.

We believe there is no bad time to buy solid investments in good index funds, which are essentially an investment in the American economy. The American way of creating prosperity is here to stay. Steady, consistent, regular, and planned purchases of a slice of America are what will make you rich.

You can't hope to predict what the market will do next. All you can figure is that, over time, it goes up twice as often as it goes down. It's like playing a slot machine rigged in your favor (you dreamer!). What would you do? Play mechanically as often as you could. The same thing holds in the stock market: play early and play often.

This is what investing in index funds allows you to do. Take your time. Stay the course.

Step 9: Avoid Costs . . . at All Costs

All waste gives my competitor the edge.

Victor Niederhoffer, market speculator and author

I (Wayne) ran index funds for several years, and it took me a long time to figure out why my fund was so strong in performance.

The experience was perplexing, strange. It was like the slowest kid in school scoring all the touchdowns; the nitwit accepted to medical school. Like an addition to the Sermon on the Mount: blessed are the simple-minded, for they shall outperform.

Managers of big mutual funds are continually running uphill in a mostly futile attempt to acquire the Big Winners. In a version of the tortoise-and-hare story, the plodding index fund gets there slow and steady—without the risk of picking a mutual fund manager whose performance goes sour.

For the past twenty-five years I've made my living studying the effects of cost on investment performance. Without getting overly technical, I'm convinced that high operating costs are a relentless enemy of good performance. Unfortunately, many active mutual fund managers dismiss cost control as unimportant compared to improving stock selection. (A well-known mutual fund manager told me, "I pick stocks; the rest is just plumbing.") The historical record shows that turning on the faucet full blast isn't going to give you better water pressure if the pipe has a steady leak.

There are many good index funds, and the core of any strategy is a plain old vanilla S&P 500 fund. There are a lot of them out there but they're not all alike. Pick one that has:

- No sales charges. Believe it or not, some funds charge you to invest your own money in your own account. They pay this money out to the broker who recommends you to the fund. Since you won't be using a broker, you don't need to pay this charge.

- A rock-bottom administration fee. The fund charges you fees for accounting for your account and for performing the management. Index funds usually have fees less than 0.25 percent (that's $2.50 for each $1,000 invested), while ordinary mutual funds charge much higher fees.

- A simple strategy of matching the index without any fancy bells or whistles. You don't want to invest in an index fund in which some manager intervenes and trics to tweak the fund to make it perform better. After all, avoiding the pitfalls of human error is one of the built-in advantages of an index fund.

In a following chapter, called Picking an Index Fund, we'll provide you with a list of index funds that meet all of the above criteria. But if you want to do some research on your own and learn more about index funds, a good place to find information is on www.indexfunds.com. If you don't have access to the Internet, you could also take a look at a book by Richard E. Evans and Burton Malkiel, titled *Earn More (Sleep Better): The Index Fund Solution*.

In another chapter, The One-Piece Puzzle, we'll demonstrate how costs gobble up investment performance. But first, we have a couple of performance killers to identify.

Step 10: Avoid Taxes

I'm proud to be paying taxes in the United States. The only thing is, I could be just as proud for half the money.

Arthur Godfrey, *radio comedian*

So far we haven't talked about the biggest destroyer of investment success: Taxman. Taxman wants to take a bite at the beginning, along the way, and at the end. Let's look at each separately.

In the Beginning

The more assets you start with, the faster the returns will build up assets for you. As we mentioned earlier, tax-saving vehicles such as IRAs, Roth IRAs, and 401(k)s are especially helpful.

The table to the right shows, for different tax brackets, how much more you have to earn to invest $179 a month.

Tax Bracket (Federal, State, & Local)	Monthly Pre-tax Income Required
0%	$179
10%	$199
20%	$224
30%	$256
40%	$298
50%	$358

If you participate in a 401(k) where your employer matches your contribution, you're in luck: free $$$! If I told you that if you show me a dollar, I'd give you another dollar for you to keep tax-free, would you say no? Of course not. So why aren't you maxing out on your 401(k) contributions?

(An aside: The same *New York Times* article we quoted in Step 1, which cited the $800 retirement funds for nonhomeowners, stated that 84 percent of Americans withdraw from their 401(k) when they change jobs. Nothing could be more disastrous to a long-term wealth-building program! As a reminder, and as we explained in Step 3, by not rolling those earned funds into another 401(k) or an IRA within sixty days, you would have to pay taxes on the withdrawn funds—and whatever discipline and success you might have accumulated would be destroyed.)

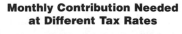

**Monthly Contribution Needed
at Different Tax Rates**

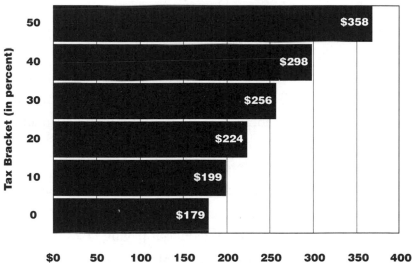

Along the Way

If you sell assets, you owe taxes on all gains on what you sold. Even if you're invested in a mutual fund, gains on what the manager sells create taxes for you (unless you've invested in tax-free retirement funds). Assets taxed away cannot grow to meet your goals.

At the End

This book won't dip deeply into this swamp, but when you succeed in growing small monthly payments into a million dollars, you have to figure out how to liquidate it without a tax gouge. You'll need a good tax attorney or tax accountant. And you'll be able to afford one by then—you'll be a millionaire!

Uncle Sam, by the way, is a notorious spender, congenitally unable to save. Think of him as the first 125 percent mortgage borrower, struggling to pay the interest on excess consumption. So don't believe the hoo-ha about Social Security trust funds—it isn't there. The only thing there, is an obligation for the next generation to support your retirement—just like you paid for your parents' Social Security, only your kids' obligation is much bigger.

The Internal Revenue Service Code is so long and complex we could easily write a ten-thousand-page explanatory thesis on what it's all about. And then we would need an additional twenty thousand pages of footnotes to explain the first ten thousand pages.

So don't even bother. Stick with the basics and avoid paying for as long as you can. Keep investing your money in a good, solid index fund and forget about paying taxes until you or your heirs cash out your estate. At that time, hire a good accountant who specializes in estate taxation, and if the estate is large enough (in excess of $1,000,000) you will probably need a tax attorney. A good tax attorney can be pure gold and help you minimize that tax bite to within the limits of the law.

Under no circumstances do we advocate cheating. If you are a solid, saving citizen, cheating is not necessary. Furthermore, honesty will help you sleep better. But if the name of the game is *delay,* we're all for it.

So buy and hold, or trade up, legally, and delay that tax payment for as long as you can. Any money not taxed away continues working for you.

Step 11: Never Sell

The important thing is to keep the important thing the important thing.

Albert Einstein, genius

An important thing to be aware of: Somewhere along the way you're going to be scared by the level, wobbliness, or plunge of the market. The second-hardest challenge you're going to face—after starting the program—is the mad desire to bail out when things look way out of line.

Our tortoise strategy is designed to map out the course ahead of time, so you know where you're going and can stay on track instead of bouncing from one plan of action to another. A key element to the success of the strategy is the long-term benefit of taking risk. Risk means your assets will go up in value and they will go down. Let us repeat the most important part of that sentence: *they will go down.* The desire to bail out will be as natural to you as extending your arms to catch yourself in a fall. Resist!

You need to ride out the bumps. If you sell when things look their worst, you won't be positioned for the randomly occurring spurts of growth as assets surge from the bottom.

Don't kid yourself, this is a tough, psychological battle and one that you must win repeatedly. When stocks are down 30 percent and portfolio managers are jumping off bridges, you must sit tight—but don't expect to be comfortable.

Here's what's going to happen to you:

First: Volatility. Your investment value is going up and down like a runaway roller coaster, with occasional frightening drops.

Second: Vulnerability. Oh, my God, this isn't a carnival ride. We're talking about retirement money—*my* retirement money!

Third: Vexation. I don't know what to do, but stopping the madness looks a lot safer than sticking with it. Sell! Sell!

Don't do it! If you try to time the market, you set yourself up for a double mistake. First, you may sell early, when there's much more to be earned by staying invested. Then, once you're out, you face the opposite problem: deciding when to get back in. That's another chance for a big mistake.

We want to emphasize the dangers of follow-your-emotions investing. To do this, we'll draw a simulated stock-price roller coaster going down and up, down and up, as in the chart below. Let's look at some emotionally significant points on the curves.

The Emotional Buying Strategy

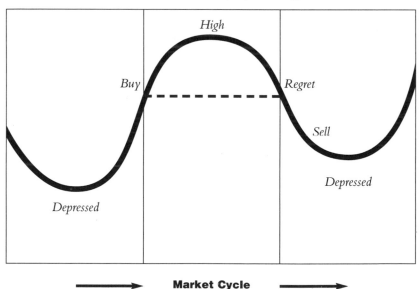

Start with *Depressed*. At this point in the market, prices are down and so are investors. It's the darkest hour; doom and gloom abound. Nobody wants to buy stocks.

As the market turns and begins to pick up, investors will overcome their gloom and begin to *Buy*. A few will react quickly as prices first turn upward, but the emotional investor will need a lot of confirming trend before he or she is encouraged to buy at this point on the roller coaster. Late buyers, either because of fright, skepticism, or inattention, might buy at even higher prices.

All these buyers will be patting themselves on the back all the way to the *High* point of the market. But how many of these buyers will recognize this as a top point? Not many, we'd bet. More likely they will ride it back down, hoping all the way that the fall is only temporary. They will tell themselves they were playing with the market's money, not their own, as though you couldn't buy a bag of potatoes with market gains.

Down we ride the market until we hit the point of *Regret*. Why regret? Note the dashed line shows that *Regret* is at the same price level as *Buy*. As the price falls through *Regret,* our investors now experience losses of their own money. Will they sell? Not much chance. They will be emotionally vested in the stock, which was once worth the *High* price and could go up that high again. But, for now, *High* stands for *hope*. These investors will hang on until all hope is lost.

As prices continue to plummet, fear will set in, triggering a *Sell* near the *Depressed* point.

Pity our poor emotional investor. The net result of riding this emotional roller coaster was to *Buy* at the point indicated on the left, and *Sell* at the point indicated on the right—with a net loss of the buy price less the sell price. What you will hear then are loud wails about how the market is rigged against the little guy and that the government ought to take it over and protect the citizenry against these thieves.

What we really experienced was a swirl of greed blended in with a swirl of fear, all mixed together in a big bowl of ignorance. This is no way to accumulate a fortune.

The tortoise strategy is designed to counteract that all-too-human reactivity.

If you invest the same number of dollars when prices are low as when they are high, you will buy more low-priced shares and fewer high-priced shares; the term for this is "dollar cost averaging." The bar below the rollercoaster line shows that the tortoise investor buys more shares when prices are near the bottom and fewer when prices are at the top levels.

The Buy-Every-Month Tortoise Strategy

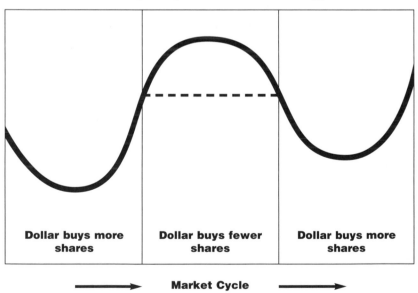

Looking at a chart of the market, the peaks and valleys are as clear as the Rockies backlit by a cloudless sunrise. Imagine standing so you could only see the left half of the peaks. Could you tell what the next peak looks like? Of course not. It's even worse in the market. Professionals have a devil of a time with market timing, and you're just an amateur. In truth, the market drops are always unexpected, sudden, sharp, and beyond our control.

The good news is that you are not at a disadvantage compared to the professionals. They have to prove themselves daily. You can prove yourself over decades. Better to stay invested and ride through the rough spots.

I have a way of dealing with financial terror that works for me. Remember when you were very young and your parents took you to a movie with some scary parts? What did you do? What I did was to cover my eyes and not watch.

It worked for me then and it works for me now—I don't look at my account very often. Once every year or two is plenty, believe it or not. I don't want to be tempted to *do* something. If you try to match frequency of action to frequency of information, your broker or Taxman, not you, will end up the millionaire.

If your 401(k) has a Web site or a twenty-four-hour phone line where you can check constantly on your account's value, *don't!* Alternative: do it every February 29, without fail.

I owned my last house—sold to me by Winnikoff—for nineteen years, through several California real estate cycles. The value went up, down, up, who knew what next? The point is that the market value wasn't really important, *because I wasn't intending to sell!* When the kids grew up and left home, we moved to a smaller, more convenient house. Only then was the market value important. The same principle applies to your long-term investment program. What matters is where you are at the end, not the path you took to get there.

Remember, this is a very conservative strategy, designed to accumulate value over time at low cost and tolerable fluctuations. You're not betting on individual stock decisions, so you shouldn't be vulnerable to the high anxiety that haunts stock pickers. The *process* is all you need, and believing in it—because it makes sense—will keep your focus on the goal. You're in for the long haul. You're on cruise control. Autopilot. You're in charge, you have things set up right, and it's working out fine. Even when it doesn't seem so.

If, despite all our reassurances and words of caution, your desire to sell becomes an obsessive, uncontrollable urge, at least promise yourself not to bail out all at once in a panic. Instead— if you must sell—do it in reasonable increments rather than dumping your entire investment at once. A prudent way to go about it would be to make small changes, say 10 percent of your portfolio at a time, spaced out at least two months apart, and move that small amount to a different type of investment. Making changes larger than that could lead to your thrashing about, trying to respond to your forebodings caused by every market move. And, as you know, the market changes its mood quite frequently.

Step 12: Don't Talk to Anyone About Your Investing— and Never Listen to Braggarts

Showing off is the idiot's substitute for being truly interesting.

Steve Martin in the movie L.A. Story

We're serious. Talking to others is dangerous. They will try to convince you to do what they do, and they don't know what you know. They will spin tales of quick returns that will make you drool. They've even been known to fudge the answers or tell outright lies.

- Playing the market can be hypnotic fun, but we're not doing this for fun. We're out to accumulate serious money and we're going to do it tortoise style. If you want to have some fun with some money you're willing to lose, go ahead. It can be fun and it's educational as well—as long as you never deviate from your core strategy of making contributions every single month into the index fund of your choice. If you want to have some fun on the side by playing the market, don't rob your index fund contributions to do it. Use other money.

> **Chasing stock market luck or hunches will not make you a millionaire.**

- You're not out to impress anyone. You aren't going to have the great cocktail party stories of how you bought Amazon.com and turned it into a Porsche in two weeks. Remember the old poker player's saying: Winners laugh

and tell jokes. The losers, who vastly outnumber the winners, are silent. Or liars. After all, why should they advertise
their failures? So don't be swept away by seductive tales of
instant riches; you might as well go to the racetrack or buy
that lottery ticket. Remember though: the newspapers never
announce the names of the losers, who are legion.

- Skip the flavor-of-the-month investment. There's always
  something new and immensely clever, but you don't want
  to take on the risk and anxiety levels. You're running a
  marathon, not a sprint.

  Ignore this advice and here's what happens. First, a far-
  fetched performance oddity turns into envy: *Look how rich
  I'd be!* Then, regret kicks in: Why didn't *I* buy that? *They
  know more than I do!* Look out, because you know what
  comes next: greed. *I want it, and I want it now!* Then delu-
  sion: *I can do this year what they did last year!* Next thing you
  know, you're driving eighty miles an hour down the high-
  way with your eyes firmly fixed on the rearview mirror.
  Soon your patient investment program crashes on a sharp
  and unexpected turn.

- Don't listen to those who have something to gain from
  changing your behavior. Don't invest with "that seductive
  young man or woman" from the brokerage firm. Remember:
  Costs are evil. He or she brings evil.

- There are always people on the other end of the phone line
  who want to take your money, although that's the last thing
  they would ever say to you. Ignore them. *Never, never, never
  respond to any financial offer from an unsolicited phone call.* Give
  me an N! Give me an E! Give me a V, an E, an R. What
  does it spell? N–E–V–E–R !

- There is one more question you should ask yourself yearly: Is there a reason for me to save and invest more? (Needless to say, don't opt for less.)
- Ignore the current events in the financial press and on television. What you're doing is not newsworthy and current events are just a sideshow, pure entertainment. But not pure life. Watching your million dollars become a pure reality will be far more satisfying as the years go by.
- Don't be derailed by great performance numbers on individual stocks or funds. The numbers are *precise,* but not *accurate* in a way that can help you make decisions for the future. Sure XYZ fund was the best-performing fund from Halloween to St. Swithin's Day, and that's a joyous fact for them, but *irrelevant* to you; you've already missed that glorious ride. It might have been skill, but far more likely it was luck. *Chasing stock market luck or hunches will not make you a millionaire.*

  The winning strategy is always to keep the maximum amount of assets at work.
- Humorist Josh Billings once said, "It ain't what you don't know that hurts you, it's what you know that ain't so." One of the hidden advantages of indexing is that it keeps you from overconfidence. It's the overconfidence that leaves you prone to action—action that probably can't help you and could quite possibly hurt you.

  So think twice before you allow yourself to be influenced by someone who's bragging about his latest big score in the stock market and urging you to go for it too. Ask yourself whether your buddy's overconfidence today really reflects the big picture. Does his strategy take into account the costs and the effects those costs would have on your net profit? Is his talk only about those big scores—which are easy to remember and fun to relish—but never about the inevitable bum choices—which are depressing and all too easily forgotten?

When you admit you don't know anything (and who but a self-acknowledged tortoise would pursue a strategy like this?), you have the advantage of humility—a quality that is much more likely to make you a millionaire than overconfidence ever will.

Picking an Index Fund

The shortest route to top quartile performance is to be in the bottom quartile of expenses.

Jack Bogle, founder of Vanguard

For the tortoise investor the index fund has all the key attributes we want:

- Long-haul stocks
- Massive diversification
- Low cost—low fee, low tax

As our standard of comparison, we're going to use the Vanguard 500 Index Fund. This is a fund that meets all our criteria, and it is the first and most well-known of all the index funds. To set the record straight, however, there are many similar funds that would do as well.

The following table is an excerpt from indexfunds.com's list of Large Blend Index Funds, which includes funds that meet the criteria we suggest, plus a couple with slightly higher costs.

Fund Name	Symbol	Expense Ratio	Minimum Starting Balance
Vanguard 500	VFINX	0.18%	$3,000
USAA S&P 500 Index	USSPX	0.18%	$5,000
Fidelity Spartan Market	FSMKX	0.19%	$10,000
Dreyfus BASIC S&P 500	PEOPX	0.20%	$2,500
California Inv Tr S&P 500	SPFIX	0.20%	$5,000
SSGA S&P 500	SVSPX	0.22%	$10,000
Deutsche 500 Index[5]	BTIEX	0.25%	$2,500
Transamerica Premier	TPIIX	0.35%	$1,000
Schwab S&P 500 Select	SWPIX	0.35%	$2,500

We've sorted these funds by expense ratio, which is the amount the fund management company charges you per year to manage your money.

Managing the Minimum Balance Requirement

See the column labeled Minimum Starting Balance? The funds set these minimum balances to keep them from having to service very small accounts. It's no surprise, then, that the lower the minimum balance, sometimes the higher the fee.

We've suggested a monthly savings program of, for example, $179 a month, which is lower than the minimum balance required. What can you do?

- If you have as little as $1,000 available in the bank, you could kick-start your program by opening an account

---

[5]Despite the European name, this is an S&P 500 index fund managed by a U.S. subsidiary of the German bank.

with Transamerica Premier. If you have a spare $3,000 you could start in the lower-fee Vanguard fund. By doing that you would accelerate along your path to millionairedom.

- If you have less than $1,000 in readily available funds, you can set the money aside in a bank account for a few months until you accumulate the minimum. You won't get the market returns, of course, until you actually invest in the index fund, but you will get the process started. If you take this course of action, you need to exercise a little extra discipline.

  One way to increase your discipline is to use one of the automatic savings plans that many banks offer. They will automatically transfer a set amount from your checking account to your savings account every month. Do not think of the money you set aside here as a "nest egg" fund to tap for emergencies. This is the start of your family fortune.

  As soon as you have enough money accumulated, send it off to one of the fund companies listed on pages 153 and 154. From that point forward, you can send a monthly check or, better yet, an automatic transfer directly to your index fund.

- If you invest in one of the higher-fee funds because of the minimum balance, it will be worth your while to move those funds to a lower-fee fund when you've accumulated a large enough balance.

Buyer Beware:
All Index Funds Are Not Alike!

An ideal index fund has but one goal: to deliver the returns of the index it's designed to track. The methods for building and running an index fund are well known. In theory, then, all index funds that track the S&P 500 should generate the same performance.

Unfortunately, as the following story shows, that's not always true. And there can be a *big* difference.

As I was putting the finishing touches on this chapter, my favorite little bank sold itself to a megabank thousands of miles away, and what had been free checking suddenly became a significant expense. Don't worry, they told me, we have a special program. You can have free checking as long as you keep $10,000 in a mutual fund. And, yes, they have an S&P 500 index fund. This sounded great.

But . . . this turned out to be no ordinary index fund, as far as expenses were concerned. First they demanded 5.25 percent of my investment as a front-end sales charge.

The fees, from their prospectus, read as follows:

Management fees	**0.70%**
Distribution and service (12[b]-1)[6] fees	**0.25%**
Other expenses	**0.19%**
Total	**1.14%**

They offered a "voluntary fee waiver" which reduced the 1.14 percent fee to 0.60 percent. Of course the prospectus also stated that "fee waivers may be discontinued at any time."

Okay, let's take a close look at this offer. Suppose I were to take this "free checking" offer for twenty years. Let's also say

---

[6]A 12(b)-1 fee is an annual charge that funds are permitted to deduct from fund assets to pay for distribution and marketing costs. In other words, you have to pay for ads so the management company can sell the fund to new shareholders. Doesn't seem quite fair, does it?

that returns averaged 10 percent per year for the next twenty years.

How much would my account be worth in twenty years? Here's how to do the computation:

1. First take away the 5.25 percent sales charge from the $10,000, leaving me $9,475 to invest.
2. Multiply this amount by 10 percent and add back the principal. At the end of the first year my investment would be worth $10,395.
3. Subtract the fee of 0.6 percent of the account balance of $10,395, which would total $62.37 for the first year.
4. Repeat steps two and three for twenty years, resulting in a final balance of $61,630. A nice number, but . . .
5. Now compare it to the Vanguard result with no sales charge and an annual 0.18 percent total fee. The comparable result: $71,255.

Over twenty years, "free" checking would cost me $9,625, averaging over $40 per month. Free checking indeed! Phooey on that. The bank would have collected $4,212 in sales and management fees. The largest portion of the cost would have come from the fact that at the end of each year I would have had less to invest because of the higher fees.

It could have been worse though. If they stopped voluntarily waiving the fee down to 0.60 percent and brought it back up to 1.14 percent, I would end up with $54,986 and the twenty-year loss would be $16,269—almost $68 per month on average.

The moral of the story is this: When selecting an index fund you want to avoid (1) any sales charges and (2) total operating expenses in excess of 0.35 percent. If the fund you're considering charges more than that, look elsewhere. They aren't offering you the best value, and you're now smart enough to know it!

The index funds we've listed in the table on page 110 are the ones we believe are the best and the safest. They're the ones we hope you will choose. If we had written this book a few years ago, we could end our list of funds right there. But some interesting things are happening in the world of indexing that may be of great benefit to you.

The rising popularity of index funds has led to a lot of new offerings, some of which seem to have very low fees and expense ratios. We would be cautious here, however. Some of these low initial fees may just be come-ons. As soon as the fund attracts initial shareholders, the company may institute higher fees when you aren't looking for them.

Nonetheless, we'd be remiss if we didn't tell you about the new developments in the investment world that may broaden your options for the future. We'll explore some of these new offerings in the chapter Alternative Ways of Indexing Your Portfolio.

The One-Piece Puzzle

To be the best at something consistently, you have to be economical, using the least amount of input to accomplish the greatest output.

Victor Niederhoffer, market speculator and author

Now that we've covered all of the basic concepts in the twelve-fold path to millionairedom, it's time to put it all together. This chapter is the most detailed in the book.

Now we have the chance to show you *why* this is a solid strategy that you can put into place and not worry. Reading this chapter should give you a confidence boost. It will show some of the hidden ways in which a poorly thought-out strategy results in performance-killing cost and leakage that would surely prevent you from attaining your goal of becoming a millionaire.

Let's compare the returns on the Vanguard 500 Index Fund to an actively managed fund with similar objectives. We'll use a simple procedure to select a fund. The next similar fund *alphabetically* after the Vanguard 500 Index Fund is the Van Kampen Pace A fund, a mutual fund. The Van Kampen mutual fund is a pretty average fund in terms of costs and portfolio style. Sometimes it performs well and beats the benchmark, so it makes a good side-by-side comparison to the index fund.

Now, I'm sure the people who run the Van Kampen mutual fund are well-motivated, smart as whips, and kind to small animals, but I want to show you what a challenge they're up against, to say nothing of the challenge facing their investors.

A poorly thought-out strategy results in performance-killing cost and leakage.

We'll compare investor experience in these two funds over ten years and you'll see how the index fund is simply a better strategy for a very long-haul investor.

We'll invest $1,000 per year each January 1 for ten years, looking at actual performance *after* all gains, losses, and costs.

Let's proceed to the bottom line: After ten years, how much money do you have from your $10,000 invested over that time?

Investment	10-Year Result
Vanguard 500 Index Fund	$23,385.20
Van Kampen Pace A Mutual Fund	$16,663.40
Difference	$6,751.80

Whoa! After ten years, you've made over *twice* as much investment return by investing in the index fund! Where'd the money come from?

Pure and simple: By keeping costs low, the index fund keeps your money working for you. The result over the long haul—and the longer the haul, the more dramatic the result—is that the tortoise index fund beats the actively managed hare mutual fund hands down.

We'll omit the detailed computations, but the principles are important for you to understand so that you can resist the temptations to stray from your long-term strategy. Here's where the cost differentials come in:

Sales Charges

Van Kampen's mutual fund pays 5.75 percent to the broker who sent the client to their fund. This is a service you don't need. $575 for nothing. Worse, this fee is deducted right at the start where it can't benefit you through Einstein's compounding.

Administration Fee

Vanguard's fee averages less than a quarter of Van Kampen's: 0.21[7] percent vs. 0.89 percent of your accumulated assets. Over ten years you'd have paid Vanguard $250 and the good people at Van Kampen $930—almost a full year's contribution!

Transaction Costs

This is perhaps the greatest and most evil cost. It's hard to see this cost directly, but we can see its effect in the performance

---

[7]Since this calculation was made, Vanguard has reduced their fee even further, to 0.18 percent, which is the percentage that appears in the chart on page 110.

figures. The Vanguard 500 Index Fund averaged 18.4 percent return per year, compared to Van Kampen's 15.5 percent.

Either the Van Kampen people are abysmally dumb, something we don't believe, or what they're paying to trade is eating up the value of stock research. We have a lot of support for the excessive transaction cost explanation, but it requires a more complex calculation than we need to go into here.

The bottom line is that the difference between Vanguard's annual 5 percent turnover (buying and selling stocks in the portfolio) and Van Kampen's 40 percent to 200+ percent turnover, multiplied by well-documented transaction cost measures, accounts for the lion's share of the difference in performance. The Van Kampen people may not have thought of this.[8]

Taxes

Because of high turnover, Van Kampen's mutual fund generates income and capital gains on which you then have to pay taxes, unless your funds are in their 401(k) or an IRA. Over the ten years, these taxes come to $870 for the index fund and $3,510 for the Van Kampen mutual fund. $3,510 is more than one-third of the contributions into the fund.

Just to add insult to injury, Taxman makes the mutual funds distribute this as taxable income every year—even though you haven't realized any income! It seems terribly unfair, but the government is smart enough to figure out that you can't collect taxes from people who don't have money. Once you become

---

[8]If you need a sure cure for insomnia, try reading some of the commentaries on www.plexusgroup.com.

a systematic saver, you automatically become a target to the government. Sorry about that.

Uninvested Funds

Van Kampen managers keep cash in the mutual fund to pay out exiting shareholders and to seize hot opportunities. Van Kampen keeps something like 2.3 percent cash, which is low by industry standards. Vanguard, in contrast, keeps a super-low 0.6 percent cash. Vanguard estimates that this cash drag costs the average mutual fund about 0.7 percent per year. While this doesn't seem like a whole lot, it builds up *relentlessly* over long periods.

Remember, you're investing for the next ten, twenty, thirty, even fifty years. There's a good chance that the genius mutual fund manager will die, retire, or fail long before *you're* ready to cash out. Why would you think that his number-two guy is as good as he is? Index funds, on the other hand, are run unemotionally by machines called computers. They don't get old (oh, really?), go senile, or go postal. They just mechanically do what they're told: own the whole market, all the time, at nearly zero cost.

Well, that's the whole case.[9] Sure, every year there are some mutual fund managers who outperform the index. Unfortunately, they're seldom the same managers year after year and, with seven thousand mutual funds available, searching for the right one is a needle-in-a-needlestack problem. Since we're going to stay invested for a long time, accepting the humdrum but low-cost index fund is a safer, easier bet.

----

[9]There's an interesting mutual fund cost calculator put together by the Securities and Exchange Commission at www.sec.gov that you can use for free. It doesn't figure in taxes or turnover costs, but it's fun to play with.

An Amazing Secret!

Isn't it amazing how difficult it is to be mediocre!

Paul Samuelson, Nobel Laureate in economics

By now you should have figured out that you can compete with the pros with a simple strategy.

It turns out that you have a lot of help in making your strategy work, from a most unexpected source—those seven thousand–plus mutual funds, five thousand–plus registered investment advisors, and over half a million registered representatives and investment consultants. The pros themselves! They're your silent partners, although they won't admit it because they don't want you to know about it. Because if you knew about it, you wouldn't be needing the high-priced services they offer.

Here's how it works.

What happens when Pfizer comes up with a new drug like Viagra, one that opens up all sorts of human potential . . . and profit potential? Hundreds, if not thousands, of smart, eager-beaver investors and analysts try to figure out to the penny what this means for earnings, how long it will last, how the stock will react, and so on. They will stay tuned to the company news, analyze and interpret the facts, make studied decisions, and boldly take risks. They will buy Pfizer stock—and here's the key point—until they've pushed the price so high that they figure there isn't any more juice in it.

Who says there aren't any free lunches in economics!

Meanwhile you and I, not even paying attention, get to piggyback on their insights for free! Free, of course, only if you own the stock—another advantage of index fund diversification. The hotshots drive the price up and you and I ride along for free.

Who says there aren't any free lunches in economics? Amazing, isn't it?

And there's one nice feature we haven't told you about yet: It doesn't take a lot of brilliance, time, or effort on your part to maintain this strategy once it's set up. This process runs itself. In fact, if you do nothing, odds are you'll come out better than if you fret and fuss with it.

Oh, and let's keep encouraging all those professional analysts and portfolio managers to continue working hard. That's what keeps us tortoises from having to work up a sweat.

Any Flaws I Need to Be Aware Of?

Penetrating so many secrets, we cease to believe in the unknowable. But there it sits nevertheless, calmly licking its chops.

H. L. Mencken, American humorist

This is a great strategy, but like any plan—investment or otherwise—it's not a sure thing.

You're not going to wake up on February 18, 2036, or whenever, and find that your account balance just reached $1,000,000. It might be sooner, and it might be later. It might go above, then fall below. If we were to go through a very long economic depression, World War III, famine, pestilence, or plague, you might not make it within your time frame.

> **After all, nothing in the future is certain.**

After all, nothing in the future is certain. There are some things no one can predict and little anyone can do about them anyway. (The asteroid is coming! The asteroid is coming! Or, as investor Chicken Little said, "Sell sky! Sell sky!")

Barring the totally unimaginable, the long-term index fund strategy is designed to maximize the chance of your becoming a millionaire regardless of the path of returns taken to get there.

Alternative Ways of Indexing Your Portfolio

It is not the strongest of the species that survive, nor the most intelligent, but the one most responsive to change.

Charles Darwin

Well, at this point you know the whole story. However, new chapters are unfolding all the time. There are new developments in the world of indexing, and we're going to tell you about them in this chapter.

But before we start, we'd like to make our position clear: Some of the following options might look very tempting to you, even more tempting than the chart of recommended index funds we showed you on page 110. Nevertheless, we stand by those recommendations.

Once indexing took off—and it *has* taken off in a big way—other management companies were salivating to compete. After all, running an index fund is a pretty simple thing. Any manager who could reduce the cost of providing the index fund would find a ready market.

Now, it's hard to beat Vanguard. Twenty-five years ago their low costs shocked the professional money management industry, which was accustomed to garnering fees two to ten times those of the Vanguard index fund. Even so, Vanguard has its own set of vulnerabilities.

Vanguard's problem is that while running the index fund takes a handful of people, taking care of the accounts of the shareholders requires an army of clerks. Envelopes must be opened, account data must be entered, deposits must be made, statements must be prepared and mailed, and so on. While the Vanguard people are astonishingly frugal compared to most fund companies, these expenses still add up. So anyone who can find ways to reduce these costs can compete directly with Vanguard's greatest strength. And people are busy as bees trying to do just that:

- A February 18, 2000, posting on indexfunds.com proclaimed that "State Street Global Advisors plans to drop fees on its S&P index fund below those of Vanguard, according to a recent SEC filing." This is no fly-by-night outfit; State Street Global is the largest money manager in the U.S.
- On April 28, 2000, indexfunds.com featured an article stating that "E-bank x.com pays customers to invest. . . . One of the best deals in indexing for the small investor could well be x.com's offer to pay investors to place their money in a reputable S&P fund."

The fund would be managed by Barclays Global Investors, the world's largest institutional index fund manager. Take away the promotional aspects of the initial payment to new investors, and you can see a core idea for low-cost operations: E-banks communicate via the Internet. That means no paper statements, no stuffing of envelopes, no postal charges—it's easy to see that this can lead to true cost efficiencies, which might be worth as much as a hundred dollars a year in savings to you.

Exchange-Traded Funds

There's another index investment option that makes it easier for you to invest in smaller amounts than your designated monthly contribution. It's almost as if someone took all these index funds, cut them up real small, and wrapped them with a nice red ribbon so you could buy them the same way you would buy Philip Morris stock—one share at a time.

Well, the American Stock Exchange has done just that. They call them SPDRs ("Spiders"), which stands for Standard & Poor's Depository Receipts. They belong to an increasingly popular family called exchange-traded funds.

The operative word in exchange-traded funds is "traded." They're meant to be traded; that is, the same kind of buy-and-sell strategy you'd use for trading shares of stock. This is quite different from our recommended strategy for investing in index funds, which is a buy-and-hold strategy.

Nevertheless, Spiders sound appealing for a few reasons:

• You can buy Spiders one share at a time through any brokerage firm anytime the market's open, as opposed to an index fund which you can only buy at the end of the day.
• They cost between $20 and $30 per share, which allows you to buy into the index in tiny increments. This sounds like a solution to your "minimum starting balance" problem, doesn't it? Unfortunately, the answer is no—for cost

reasons we'll detail shortly in the disadvantages section below.

- Like the funds offered by x.com, Spiders are run by Barclays, so you have no worry here in terms of a reputable firm.
- The management fees are in line with the low-cost index mutual funds. However, there are other costs involved, as we detail below.

Offsetting the convenience of investing in Spiders are some disadvantages:

- As with trading any stock on an exchange, you pay a commission each time you buy or sell. Those commissions could run you as much as $25 per transaction, which is prohibitive for small purchases. (This is in contrast to investing in an index fund, which does not charge you a commission for buying and selling your shares in the fund.)
- Unlike index fund or mutual fund shares, you can't buy Spiders in fractions. Therefore, unless Spiders happen to be selling for $179 per share (or a figure that is evenly divisible by your monthly contribution), you'll have trouble making that monthly installment. You don't want to undercontribute, and you may not be comfortable overcontributing.
- As with any stock transaction, the exchange or the broker collects a "spread" between what buyers pay and sellers receive. This can amount to as much as 1 percent of the transaction price.

Is this worth your while? We don't think so. Aside from the cost disadvantages of Spiders, we don't like the process of focusing on trading monthly. When you contact your broker monthly, he'll try to talk you into some hot deal that he's ped-dling. Worse, the temptation to skip a month is too high, and once you get into *that* habit your program is dead, dead, dead. Better to have an automatic withdrawal you can't touch that goes directly into the index fund of your choice.

But wait. There's more. Spiders aren't the only type of exchange-traded funds available to you. Barclays Global Investors—clever people, aren't they?—have a new wrinkle called "open-ended" exchange-traded funds that will sell for even lower fees; they estimate 0.08 percent to 0.12 percent.

> **We don't know what tomorrow's headlines might bring.**

This is not only much lower than the Spiders' fee, but it's also well below Vanguard's 0.18 percent fee for its index fund. That lower fee, however, would be offset by the same disadvantages that Spiders have—a commission fee, a spread, and your inability to buy them in fractions.

So what's Vanguard doing to counter this new competi-tion? Well, they're not taking it lying down. On May 13, 2000, the *Los Angeles Times* ran a report headed "To Counter Bar-clays, Vanguard Will Offer Exchange-Traded Funds."

Okay, so we've given you a lot of news and facts. But what you'd really like to know right now is: How does all this affect *my* investment strategy?

The straight answer is, it doesn't. At least not for now.

We felt that we needed to explain these things to you, because you're sure to hear of them once you start tuning into investing and index funds. But we cannot recommend that you use them now to execute your tortoise-millionairedom strategy.

Our advice is to go for one of the tried-and-true funds on the chart on page 110, and wait at least three years before contemplating a change. By then, your dedicated authors will have had sufficient time to analyze these new funds and determine their true cost effectiveness. After all, Vanguard's been in business for twenty-five years and hasn't raised its fees in all that time. The others have also worked hard to squeeze expenses so they can be competitive with their fee schedules.

We simply can't guarantee that these new funds' fees aren't just too good to be true and won't soon be raised to something higher than Vanguard's. Besides, everything points to Vanguard cutting its costs even more in order to compete with these newcomers. They simply don't have any other choice.

Where do all these new developments end? As authors, we have a dilemma: we don't know what tomorrow's headlines might bring. We will certainly see aggressive competition to bring in assets. And we can expect price wars to snare customers for start-up index funds. The well-established fund companies are not going to let competitors steal their customers without a fight. We would expect to see them counter any true cost-cutting moves with features of their own.

All in all, this is a wonderful thing for you as a long-term index fund investor. Low costs keep the money in your account working for you. Intense competition to trim excess costs can only work to your benefit. If one of these new funds turns out to deliver a significant cost advantage to you, it may make sense to switch. But please make sure you don't upset the process in the meantime.

Here's our promise to you, dear readers: We will watch what happens for you, and post our findings and opinions on the Worldwide Web at lunchmoneymillionaire.com. Here you will be able to read whatever new information we will have accumulated. If you're not online, you can write to us in care of our publisher, and we'll send you the latest information.

End Games

How old would you be if you didn't know how old you was?

Satchel Paige, baseball pitcher

What happens near the end of a football game when one team is ahead and controls the ball? When the game's won, there is no more reason to take risk. The quarterback takes the snap of the ball and kneels down, to make sure that the clock runs out with his team still winning.

Down the road you may want to take a similar strategy. At some point you may want to declare victory and call it quits. This may happen earlier or later than you expected, or events in your life may dictate that taking risk no longer fits into your plans.

If your goal was to pass the money on to your children, there's less urgency about reducing the risk. Yes, the value might fluctuate. But if you sell, Taxman is going to gorge himself at your expense. It's probably better to pass the assets on to your heirs.

As we said earlier, you'll need professional help. Get a good attorney or accountant. Dealing with the complexities of estates and taxes is beyond our call here. We've boasted that this strategy takes no brilliance and no hard work. But dodging Taxman probably takes both.

We've been demonizing Taxman perhaps unfairly. Taxman and Taxwoman are civil servants. They hate being ridiculed, falsely accused of mental deficiencies and evil intent. They work and do a job just like the rest of us. Treat them well and they will generally reciprocate with good and helpful behavior. Scream and yell at them and you get what you deserve. Taxman is simply following the legal orders of the government. For most of them it's just a job, with too-low pay but great government benefits and security.

The real power of taxation resides in the bosom of government. The government is coming to realize that estate taxes, like many other taxes, tend to punish good behavior. Make a million in one year and Taxman, under the wrong circumstances, can take about half. But leave an *estate* of a million and much of it is tax-exempt. In the near future it may all be tax-exempt.

The so-called new economy of the twenty-first century has given us a new twist. The conservatives are talking about more government spending while the liberals are talking about tax cuts. The try-to-please-everyone political philosophies are aimed at the eighty million Americans who own stock and *vote in every election.*

These savvy voters want to keep their hard-earned estates intact and do not want Taxman as an overbearing partner. Many big, big rich people take their earnings abroad, paying low, low taxes in places like Liechtenstein and Switzerland. Uncle Sam now has stiff tax competition from abroad. So Taxman is under attack from above, below, and across the desk. That's likely to be good news for you.

The best way to reduce market risk is to reduce exposure to the stock market by selling shares in the index fund which served you so well and putting the assets into less volatile, interest-paying bonds. Your fund company will likely have a bond portfolio, even an indexed bond portfolio, available to you for this very purpose.

Warning: whenever selling assets, be careful of Taxman's voracious appetite! Taxman doesn't care that you are transacting to preserve assets for your retirement. Taxman only sees an opportunity to increase tax revenues. It's important to use your tax-free retirement assets first to make these risk adjustments.

As for converting the assets to cash, it's a snap. You just write a letter to the fund company asking them to write a check in the amount you want. They would even be happy to send you a check out of your account every month if you're using it for living expenses.

One caution: at age sixty-five you could easily have another twenty years to live. Since Social Security was put in place, life expectancy has increased fifteen years. Who knows what miracles of medical research will lengthen our lives in the future? With all the miracles available from the decoding of the human genome, researchers may find the keys that unlock some of the secrets of aging.

With twenty years of retirement, you almost have time for another long-term tortoise investment program! With improvements in geriatric medicine, you might even have time for two programs!

Now let's stop focusing on yourself for a minute and think about your children. Unless you spend that money yourself, or will it to someone else, your children will inherit your fortune. Have you prepared them for that?

Right now I want you to go to the kitchen and get *The Joy of Cooking* off the shelf. That's right, the cookbook. (We said this book was about cooking up a fortune!) Now turn to the dedication page, which is two pages behind the title page. Do you see what it says? It quotes Goethe's *Faust:* "That which thy fathers have bequeathed to thee, earn it anew if thou wouldst possess it." Once we get beyond the outdated language, we see that the *Joy of Cooking* authors are trying to tell us that cooking is a skill that must be learned anew by every generation.

Assuredly, none of us is born knowing how to cook, much less how to manage and nurture a million dollars. *You* will have learned money discipline yourself by following the simple strategy laid out in this book, or you wouldn't be a millionaire. But have your children learned it?

If they're at all observant, and you haven't kept the whole thing a secret from them, you probably have been teaching them good spending habits day by day without even knowing it. We would hope that you taught them when they were young how to save and how to spend some money for their own joy, satisfaction, and motivation.

Suppose, however, that you thought it would be better if they had no inkling of the wealth you have accumulated. Certainly they would be pleasantly surprised when your will is read, but that's not the point. *You* have behaved responsibly for years, and you owe it to them to pass on that same virtue along with the money. If they know nothing about saving and spending responsibly, when the lawyer reads your will it'll be too late. You didn't save systematically for decades so they could blow it all in a year or two.

We're sure you get the point: Your family can accumulate wealth over many generations—*but only if they know how.* It's your job to teach them. Start now.

Congratulations!
You're on Your Way!

The longest journey begins with a single step.

Chinese proverb

You now know all you need to know to become a millionaire. What's keeping you poor is the unwillingness to make a very long-term commitment.

There may be obstacles in the future that you can't surmount. Serious health problems could keep you from fulfilling your plan. Even then, wouldn't you be more comfortable with a pile of money in the bank?

Now, can you remember the first step? Call the fund company and set up that automatic transfer. You'll be amazed at how good you feel about yourself in a decade or two.

Or . . .

What do you mean you haven't done it?

Nothing happens until *you* take that first step. *Do it now!* And if that fails . . .

Turn to page one and read this book again! This time, read slo-o-owly. Make sure you understand the content and purpose of every chapter before you move on.

Oh, just one last reminder: *Never sell.*

Afterword

When you sell a man a book, you don't sell him twelve ounces of paper and ink and glue—you sell him a whole new life.

Christopher Morley

Well, we've done all we can. It's up to you now. We know you want to do what's right for you and your family.

But we can't reach out of this book and take you by the hand, though we would if we could.

We've been where you are right now, on the threshold of saying good-bye to financial worries and hello to prosperity. Each of us has started his own business and we know how difficult it is to take that first step. Yet without that launch, nothing ever happens. Don't do anything and in ten years you'll be in the same position you are now, only with ten years of useless guilt piled on.

So don't put your future on hold. Follow the simple directions in this book and you will be a millionaire. It's up to you whether you dump a hard-earned $85,000 into a good index fund all at once or do it over a twenty-five-year span at $805 per month. Or $179 per month for forty years. Or 97 cents per day for sixty years. But you will do it. The trick is to continue doing it. Be steady. And we assure you that the trick becomes a glorious habit after just a few months.

If you have a big hole in your economic bucket, fix it immediately. For your economic success depends on your ability to

1. **SAVE**
2. **SAVE**
3. **SAVE**

and

4. **INVEST**
5. **INVEST**
6. **INVEST**

without all those coins and paper money dropping out on someone else's economic landscape.

Why should you save? Because the brave and gutsy men and women who defied King George III at the risk of their lives did not do it just for themselves. They also did it for posterity. They did it for us. All of us.

If you think that making money has nothing to do with making our less-than-perfect world a better place, consider this: Your personal chance of making a difference, even in a small way, is infinitely greater with a million bucks in your bucket than it is if you spend 125 percent of your earnings every week and then deplore the fact that you are always broke and that's all you ever have time to think about.

Have no illusions. One million dollars is a lot of money today and will still be a lot of money a hundred years from today. You can do a lot of good with that much money—for yourself, for your family, and for the world your children will inherit.

So do not be afraid to be rich. Do not believe that money is evil. Or that *all* rich people are evil. Some rich people are actually very nice. They look at money as a tool. And when that tool is used for good purposes, money becomes a tool for making good things happen. To believe otherwise is to entice failure and negativity to stalk you in the very serious game of life. No one likes a miser who makes his or her money the agent of misery. (By the way, *miser* and *misery* come from the same Latin root word, *miser:* miserable, wretched, pitiable.)

You are much better off closing out your life as a good rich person than a bad poor one. We want you to do exactly that. This book was not written to extol greed. We wrote it to extol virtue and decency. We believe that the mysticism of the well-written word can change your life for the better. It happened *to* us and *for* us. And now it's your turn.

Save your money, invest it wisely, and the future is yours. We have an absolute faith in the future and the good that may come with it. But we also have faith in the present.

We live in a very interesting era. It is an era in which knowledge is replacing ignorance. This fact in itself puts us light-years ahead of the previous centuries in which serfs and slaves were forbidden by church and state to become literate, when the penalty for commoners learning to read and write was death. Isn't that reason enough to take the knowledge you've gained from this book and turn it into your own millionaire success story?

Believe us when we tell you that we did not write this book for money. We did not write it for glory. We took a good deal of precious time out of our high-pressure, highly demanding businesses to write it because we believe there is a need for the simple truths contained herein. But most of all, we wrote it for our readers. For you. Why? Because we believe in you. Isn't it part of our national tradition to help others just as others have helped us? We have put our entire economic life experiences into these pages and know with certainty that you will succeed in your goals just as we succeeded in ours.

Besides, no one ever asked us how to get poor. But a lot of people constantly ask us how to get rich. That singular request was one of the great incentives for writing this book. No hokum. No magic. No trickery. Just the facts. The proof. The certainty that if you follow the advice herein you will be a millionaire.

We have never laid claim to superior mystical knowledge or special magical insights. But we do know the answer to the question we are asked by people who approach us after speeches, lectures, seminars, and TV talk shows: "Do you *really* think I can become a millionaire?"

The answer is an unequivocal, absolute *yes!* We do not see financial success as the product of chance or luck. Success is the product of choice. Take our advice seriously and we know you *will* be successful. But the final choice is yours and yours alone.

We sincerely hope this book has shown you not only why you *can* do it, but also why you *must* do it. Our posterity and our traditions demand it.

The dream's in your court. Show us what you can do with it.

Thank you for reading our words. We wish you good health, much love, and great success in the attainment of your goals.

And be sure to let us know when you make your first million.

We'd like to close with a quote that one of us (Wayne) has carried with him everywhere for fifteen years.

Until one is committed, there is hesitancy, the chance to draw back, always ineffectiveness. Concerning all acts of initiative (and creation), there is one elementary truth, the ignorance of which kills countless ideas and splendid plans:

that the moment one definitely commits oneself,

then providence moves too.

All sorts of things occur to help one that would never otherwise have occurred. A whole stream of events issues from the decision, raising in one's favor all manner of unforeseen incidents and meetings and material assistance, which no man could have dreamed would have come his way.

Whatever you do, or dream you can, begin it. Boldness has genius, power and magic in it. Begin it now.

Goethe

Appendix 1: How Long Might It Take to Become a Millionaire?

What would your account be worth if you invested in an S&P 500 index fund at a 0.18 percent fee? On the following pages we present four different charts showing inital investments of four different amounts. You will see a dramatic difference in the amount of money you can accumulate.

How to Read the Tables

Each column represents a different start date, going back to the end of 1939.

The heading above the table indicates the dollars invested per month.

Each row in the column represents, in five-year increments, the dollars accumulated through saving and investing beginning at the times indicated by the column heading.

In the $111 table, for example, if you started in 1939, in the 1940s, or in the 1950s you would have been a millionaire in forty-five years. If you had started in the 1960s or 1970s—as far as our table goes—you would have accumulated your million dollars a lot faster. So the condition of the market at the time you start your program will influence how quickly or slowly you accumulate wealth.

The tables on the following pages show the results for other levels of investment.

Saving $111 per month

Years	Dec-39	Dec-44	Dec-49	Dec-54	Dec-59	Dec-64	Dec-69	Dec-74	Dec-79	Dec-84	Dec-89	Dec-94
5	9,948	8,520	12,286	9,633	9,462	7,364	5,400	8,630	9,598	10,500	3,345	12,960
10	24,715	36,641	33,859	25,169	19,179	11,782	19,066	26,405	34,296	23,961	41,611	
15	83,547	82,319	65,129	39,025	22,179	31,661	46,992	76,450	59,728	95,949		
20	175,651	145,064	89,517	39,645	52,178	71,837	128,087	123,088	220,405			
25	299,016	190,518	84,079	86,643	112,312	190,405	200,701	440,876				
30	385,042	172,962	174,326	180,300	291,924	294,369	710,943					
35	344,148	349,720	353,271	462,453	446,958	1,036,875						
40	687,522	699,272	896,304	703,274	1,567,831							
45	1,365,655	1,764,147	1,355,380	2,459,720								
50	3,435,582	2,659,803	4,728,819									
55	5,172,077	9,267,757										
60	18,009,589											

Saving $179 per month

Years	Dec-39	Dec-44	Dec-49	Dec-54	Dec-59	Dec-64	Dec-69	Dec-74	Dec-79	Dec-84	Dec-89	Dec-94
5	16,042	13,739	19,813	15,535	15,258	11,875	8,707	13,918	15,478	16,933	13,457	20,899
10	39,855	59,087	54,602	40,587	30,928	19,000	30,747	42,580	55,307	38,640	67,103	
15	134,728	132,749	105,029	62,932	35,767	51,057	75,779	123,285	96,318	154,729		
20	283,257	233,932	144,357	63,932	84,143	115,845	206,555	198,493	355,429			
25	482,197	307,232	135,587	139,721	181,115	307,050	323,653	710,962				
30	620,924	278,921	281,120	290,753	470,760	474,703	1,146,476					
35	554,978	563,962	569,690	745,757	720,771	1,672,077						
40	1,108,707	1,127,654	1,445,390	1,134,109	2,528,305							
45	2,202,273	2,844,885	2,185,702	3,966,576								
50	5,540,263	4,289,233	7,625,753									
55	8,340,557	14,945,301										
60	29,042,490											

Saving $481 per month

Years	Dec-39	Dec-44	Dec-49	Dec-54	Dec-59	Dec-64	Dec-69	Dec-74	Dec-79	Dec-84	Dec-89	Dec-94
5	43,106	36,919	53,241	41,744	41,000	31,909	23,398	37,399	41,592	45,502	36,162	56,158
10	107,097	158,777	146,723	109,064	83,107	51,056	82,621	114,420	148,618	103,831	180,315	
15	362,036	356,716	282,228	169,108	96,111	137,198	203,630	331,284	258,821	415,780		
20	761,155	628,612	387,908	171,794	226,105	311,294	555,044	533,380	955,090			
25	1,295,735	825,579	364,343	375,452	486,683	825,089	869,705	1,910,461				
30	1,668,517	749,503	755,411	781,298	1,265,003	1,275,600	3,080,754					
35	1,491,309	1,515,451	1,530,843	2,003,961	1,936,813	4,493,124						
40	2,979,263	3,030,177	3,883,982	3,047,521	6,793,935							
45	5,917,840	7,644,636	5,873,311	10,658,788								
50	14,887,522	11,525,815	20,491,549									
55	22,412,334	40,160,279										
60	78,041,551											

Saving $805 per month

Years	Dec-39	Dec-44	Dec-49	Dec-54	Dec-59	Dec-64	Dec-69	Dec-74	Dec-79	Dec-84	Dec-89	Dec-94
5	72,143	61,788	89,103	69,863	68,618	53,403	39,159	62,590	69,609	76,152	60,520	93,986
10	179,238	265,728	245,556	182,529	139,088	85,447	138,274	191,492	248,726	173,771	301,775	
15	605,902	596,999	472,335	283,019	160,851	229,614	340,795	554,436	433,162	695,848		
20	1,273,867	1,052,042	649,201	287,514	378,411	520,981	928,920	892,664	1,598,436			
25	2,168,538	1,381,685	609,763	628,355	814,512	1,380,866	1,455,536	3,197,342				
30	2,792,424	1,254,366	1,264,253	1,307,578	2,117,105	2,134,839	5,155,939					
35	2,495,849	2,536,254	2,562,014	3,353,823	3,241,454	7,519,677						
40	4,986,084	5,071,293	6,500,219	5,100,320	11,370,309							
45	9,904,077	12,794,038	9,829,555	17,838,512								
50	24,915,708	19,289,565	34,294,588									
55	37,509,208	67,212,110										
60	130,610,080											

Appendix 2:
A Directory of
Recommended Index Funds

Vanguard 500

The Vanguard Group
P.O. Box 2600
Valley Forge, PA 19482-2600
800-871-3879
www.vanguard.com

USAA S&P 500 Index

USAA Building
San Antonio, TX 78288
800-382-8722
www.usaa.com

California Inv Tr S&P 500

California Investment Trust
44 Montgomery Street, Suite 2100
San Francisco, CA 94104
800-225-8778
www.caltrust.com

SSGA S&P 500

State Street Global Asset Management
2 International Place
Boston, MA 02110
800-647-7327
www.ssga.com

Dreyfus Basic S&P 500

Dreyfus Service Corporation
144 Glenn Curtiss Blvd.
Uniondale, NY 11556
800-645-6561
www.dreyfus.com

Transamerica Premier

Transamerica Premier Funds
Transamerica Funds
P.O. Box 9232
Boston, MA 02205-0232
800-89-ASK-US
www.transamericafunds.com

Deutsche 500 Index

Deutsche Asset Management
P.O. Box 897
Pittsburgh, PA 15230-0897
800-730-1313
www.deutscheassetmgt.db.com

Fidelity Spartan Market

Fidelity Investments
82 Devonshire Street
Boston, MA 02109
800-544-8888
www.fidelity.com

Schwab S&P 500 Select

Charles Schwab & Company
101 Montgomery Street
San Francisco, CA 94104
800-435-4000
www.schwab.com

Appendix 3: Recommended Reading List

Want to know more? Before you answer that question, we want to caution you to *not* use the quest for answers as an excuse for not starting immediately. Nothing happens until you start.

So start first, and *then* read these authors for further illumination, insight, and amusement.

- Start with Jack Bogle. Jack ran Vanguard for many years and has made more arguments for indexing than you can imagine. I recommend his 1998 book, *Common Sense on Mutual Funds.*
- Richard E. Evans and Burton Malkiel wrote a book in 1998 called *Earn More (Sleep Better):The Index Fund Solution,* which contains good background materials and deeper analyses.
- In 1989 David Chilton wrote a book called *The Wealthy Barber:The Common Sense Guide to Successful Financial Planning.*

This book is highly complementary to our ideas.

- I've gained much wisdom from the columns written by Jason Zweig in *Money* magazine and those written by Jonathan Clements for the *Wall Street Journal*.

- Anything written by my good friend Peter Bernstein. Peter combines great wisdom with a profound understanding of economics and investing. I especially recommend *Against the Gods: The Remarkable Story of Risk*.

Index

About the Authors

Wayne Wagner is chairman of Plexus Group, a financial consulting firm for investment managers and pension plans, and has been involved in the investing world for forty years. His clients include American Express, IBM, General Motors, General Electric, the New York Stock Exchange, NASDAQ, the London Stock Exchange, Fidelity, Vanguard, T. Rowe Price, and the states of California, Washington, and Virginia. Wayne has written *The Complete Guide to Securities Transactions* as well as many academic and popular papers on investing. He has given over 150 talks on investing throughout the United States and all over the world. He was named 1999 Consultant of the Year by *Plan Sponsor* magazine and has been featured in *Barrons*.

Al Winnikoff is a successful Malibu realtor and real estate investor. He has published three books, including *The Land Game: How to Make a Fortune in Real Estate*. Al has made over one hundred radio and TV appearances. He has been president of the Malibu Bowl Land Investment Co., Inc., Malibu Ocean View Estates, Inc., Land Equities, Inc., and Intercontinental Equities, Inc. He was general partner of numerous real estate limited partnerships. He has been a real estate consultant to many stars of stage, screen, radio, and television, and he is a consultant to numerous major real estate corporations, both foreign and domestic.